Also by Valery Chalidze:

To Defend These Rights:
Human Rights and the Soviet Union

CRIMINAL RUSSIA

CRIMINAL RUSSIA

Essays on Crime
in the Soviet Union

VALERY CHALIDZE

Translated from the Russian
by P. S. Falla

RANDOM HOUSE

New York

English translation Copyright © 1977
by Random House, Inc.

All rights reserved under International and Pan-American Copyright Conventions. Published in the United States by Random House, Inc., New York, and simultaneously in Canada by Random House of Canada Limited, Toronto. Originally published in Russian as *Ugolovnaya Rossiya* by Khronika Press, New York. Copyright © 1977 by Valery Chalidze.

Library of Congress Cataloging in Publication Data

Chalidze, Valeriĭ N   1938–
  Criminal Russia.

  Translation of Ugolovnaĭa Rossiĭa.
  Bibliography: p.
  1. Crime and criminals—Russia. I. Title.
HV7012.C4513   364′.947   76–53467
ISBN 0–394–40598–6

Manufactured in the United States of America

9 8 7 6 5 4 3 2

First American Edition in the English language

To my friend, the remarkable Russian
counselor-at-law Sophie Kallistratova

Foreword

Crime in Russia is so vast a subject that one book cannot hope to cover all of it. I have chosen to write on those aspects that especially interest me, and I have been influenced to some extent by the availability of information. I have always been fascinated by the customs and personalities of Russian criminals, and I have tried here, among other things, to trace the relationship between the moral code of the Russian underworld and early Russian customary law.

My sources are the few available memoirs by former convicts, members of the criminal underworld, and officials of the Soviet prison system that I believe to be accurate; my own conversations with informed individuals in the Soviet Union; the published texts of statutes and judicial decisions; Soviet publications on law and sociology; and the Soviet press.

According to official Soviet propaganda, there is no professional crime and no underworld in the USSR. Crime statistics are a state secret; all that are ever released to the public are tantalizing relative statements, such as the fact that in 1955 the crime rate was lower than it was in 1928. Newspaper reports of court proceedings are scanty, and even legal scholars cannot always get access to court records. The few publications and films on crime and criminals that appear are carefully censored first to avoid "corrupting the public"—which means in this case letting the people find out the truth about crime in their midst. All crimes are attributed to survivals of capitalism sixty years after the Revolution.

Curiously, Soviet dissenters as well as Soviet officials tend to regard the criminal world as something alien to Russia. One of Solzhenitsyn's heroes says, "I don't count thieves as Russians." It is very convenient, if you love your country, to exclude from it everything you dislike. You can exclude from the Russian nation dissidents, or KGB agents, or Bolsheviks, or prostitutes, or speculators, according to your taste. But such an approach will not help you understand Russian society, which, like all societies, gives birth to and includes people of various kinds, not all of them sympathetic, but all of them members of the society.

I am also concerned in this book with peculiarly Soviet crimes—free enterprise, speculation, misappropriation of government property. The evidence indicates that these are now so prevalent that the authorities have been forced to be lenient with the culprits to avoid swamping the judicial and prison systems.

It is my hope that *Criminal Russia* will help fill some of the gaps that exist in the outside world's knowledge of life in the Soviet Union today. I have collected the material for this book over a period of many years. A number of persons in Russia, whom I shall not name here, provided me with information. Vladimir Kozlovsky, Victor Kabachnik, and Pavel Litvinov were helpful to me while I was working on the book in New York. Max Hayward offered interesting comments and helpful criticism. Strobe Talbott's critique of the original manuscript was valuable. Professor Lipman Bers and Professor Alexander Volpin gave me useful comments on the first part of the book. Helena Shtein's editorial assistance was extremely important. Finally, I am grateful to the Ford Foundation for financial support for my research on the sociology of crime in the USSR.

Valery Chalidze

New York
May 1976

Contents

CRIMINAL RUSSIA

1

The Russian Criminal Tradition

The starting point of a study of crime in any specific country is an understanding of that country's criminal tradition. By criminal tradition I mean the prevailing attitudes toward what, over the centuries, a majority of mankind has come to regard as criminal acts, such as theft, murder, rape, arson, and so on. At different stages in their history some nations may not regard some of these acts as crimes, may indeed even prescribe them; yet they remain, in the larger context, criminal, at least as far as the rest of the world is concerned.

In Russia, centuries-old attitudes toward various kinds of crime still prevail. Many of these attitudes have also been held by other peoples at earlier periods of history. Thus, in a sense, the attitudes reflect the stage of social development that Russia has attained, as well as the influence of such specifically Russian factors as geography, climate, and religion.

Throughout history, crimes against property have been the commonest way of flouting the law, and in societies in which the majority of the population is virtually without private property, there tends to be a certain tolerance toward these. Among the Russian peasantry before the

Revolution, occasional as opposed to habitual theft was regarded as a civil injury rather than a crime. If the stolen object was returned and the involved parties were reconciled, the village assembly would consider the incident closed. "Even a bishop will steal if he's hungry"; "Soldiers are beaten for everything except stealing"; "The soldier didn't steal, he only took; he's got to live, and how can he get things except by stealing?"[1] are all familiar old Russian sayings.

In previous centuries the Russian word *vor*, which now means "thief," was a generic term for a criminal or a foreign enemy. *Tat* was the word for a thief. The nineteenth-century adage, "Things have come to such a pass that if you take something from somebody's farm, they call you a vor,"* suggests that in the course of time popular feeling toward property rights became more sensitive. But although the peasants meted out severe punishment to those who stole objects of vital importance to the community, there was no uniform view of property violations. Village opinion generally condemned theft from one's own commune (*obshchina*) or its members and was fairly indulgent as far as others' property was concerned. Indeed, judging from many accounts of life at the end of the nineteenth century, the peasants actually applauded theft or swindling if the victims were outsiders. It was an accepted custom for peasants to cut wood illegally in forests belonging to landowners or the czar. According to one nineteenth-century ethnographer,† "members of the clergy did not think it wrong to buy timber and firewood stolen by peasants from Crown lands or the gentry's estates," and other reports show that the gentry, too, were not above buying stolen wood.

---

* Quoted by the nineteenth-century ethnographer Sergei V. Maximov in "National Crimes and Misfortunes," *Fatherland Notes* (1869).
  † Yakushkin, *Customary Law*, Vol. 1.

There was similar tolerance toward putting cattle to graze in privately owned fields and meadows, poaching game and fish, and collecting fruit and berries from private orchards. In the Don Cossacks' territory, a peasant in need could appropriate grain from a wealthy neighbor and promise to return it when times were better. He would simply remove the unthreshed sheaves from the field, sometimes leaving a note to the effect that he was in dire straits and would repay his debt from the next harvest.

There were many popular superstitions on how to avoid danger while committing a theft. A candle made from the fat of an unbaptized baby, for example, was said to make the inmates of a house sleep so soundly that nothing would rouse them. The hand of a corpse had similar magical properties—a belief that led to a number of cases of graverobbing and even murder. There were also less extreme measures that could be taken. It was a widespread belief that if a man succeeded in stealing on the eve of the Feast of the Annunciation, he would not be caught the rest of the year no matter how much he stole:

> It is the skillfulness of the theft and not the value of the object taken that counts. In this way peasants hope in a single night to obtain a year's insurance against punishment for illicit woodcutting. As for the object filched from a neighbor, they return it to him the next morning.[2]

According to other sources, the same superstition applied to the Eve of Saints Boris and Gleb.

In certain circumstances a stolen object was supposedly more valuable than a purchased one. In Vologda province, stolen hops were said to take root more quickly than bought ones;[3] in Yaroslavl province, it was flowers; and around Archangel, the fish called *navaga* were supposedly easier to catch with a stolen hook.[4]

In his researches into the Russian peasants' understanding of criminal law in the early twentieth century, Prince V. V. Tenishchev discovered that they by and large approved of sharp trading even when no outsiders were involved: "They will often say it is the victim's own fault for not taking sufficient care." Deception was even more acceptable when it was a case of "the biter bit." "It's no good arguing with a merchant: if I don't sprinkle water on my wool or flax [to make it heavier], he will on his, and it's better I should get more money that way than that he should."

Certain regions had customs of their own. In Orlov province it was common practice to open graves and remove clothing from corpses. This was done with a nice sense of balance between the common-sense view ("It'll only rot if you leave it there") and a sense of decency (it was wrong to take the last garment off the corpse, especially if it was a young girl: "What will she stand up in on Judgment Day?"). Opening graves for superstitious purposes—to render a vampire harmless, to bring rain, etc.—was extremely common throughout nineteenth-century Russia, although it was technically a crime.[5]

I believe that it was because the peasants never developed an adequate sense of property that they differentiated so sharply between their own and their commune's rights and those of outsiders, including the Crown and the landlords. In any case, the Russian peasant's attitude toward property rights is extremely complicated, and there have been many attempts to explain its origin. In the second half of the past century Maximov wrote:

> Anything to which labor has not been applied and which is therefore not acquired capital can be stolen without sin. Landowners' property, ever since private estates were legally sanctioned, has constituted a strong temptation, like peas and turnips growing by the roadside. . . . Anything that is the product of one's own labor, care or skill is protected, but anything belonging

to priests or landlords is on the borderline, and beyond
that the power to distinguish one's own property from
other people's grows decidedly weaker.*

A number of authorities have cited the widespread Russian belief that the land should belong to the peasants—a
belief that gave rise to the dream that some day it would be
given to them—to explain or justify the popular Russian
disregard for property rights over the forests or the fruits of
the earth. We should, however, approach such explanations
cautiously, bearing in mind that they may reflect the author's love of the peasantry more than anything else. But
there is no question that the peasants had the dream (I do
not know if they have it still), and that because of it they
were more than once exploited by criminals.

The traditional Russian attitude toward property, a tan-
gled combination of dreams, superstitions, and relics of
customary law, led to an inconsistent approach to professional criminals on the part of the people. A local thief,
receiver of stolen property, or shelterer of thieves was an
object of fear and contempt and often of savage retribution.
But large-scale brigands were heroes of popular legend,
which ascribed to them amazing exploits, rare human qualities, and above all, love of the people. The legends stressed
the fact that they robbed and killed the rich but never
harmed the poor. To be sure, robbing the poor would not
make sense for a big-time criminal, but popular wisdom did
not explore the matter that far. It was enough that the
brigand had, in fact or in the popular imagination, freed
himself from dependence on the high and the mighty of the
world and realized, in part at least, the dream of those

* Similar ideas, which are sometimes called the labor principle, have
continued to influence the development of Russian law. Andrei Tverdokhlebov, a Soviet physicist who has written on human rights,[6] suggests that
such theories may have influenced the principle in the Soviet Constitution
that "he who does not work shall not eat," and also the official Soviet
persecution of "parasites," that is, persons without full-time official employment.

condemned to earn their bread by the sweat of their brows.

This dream took the form of plundering the wealthy so that the hungry might be fed, and many Russian criminals did indeed give an attractive tinge to their careers of robbery by helping the poor, although not necessarily for the sake of the legend. In reality, they had three motives. First, protecting the poor gave them a sense of power and nobility, especially if they were among those brigands who operated beyond the range of government administration and regular troops, and to all intents and purposes, ruled over large areas. This occurred fairly frequently during the colonization of territory in southern and eastern Russia, which began in the sixteenth century. As Maximov writes:

> During the expansion of Russia, plunder and brigandage were the inevitable and logical consequences of the system of conquest, of unregulated settlement and colonization. In the south and along the Volga, outbreaks of brigandage took place again and again under the leadership of such strong and able men as Bulavin, Khlopka, Razin, Pugachev, and innumerable others.[7]

Second, brigands had a highly practical reason for keeping on good terms with the local population, for although a man may hide from the authorities, he cannot hide from the peasants; he can take refuge in the forests for a time, but sooner or later he will have to approach a village for food or shelter. To be sure, the necessary good will was often forthcoming without any special return on the robber's part; in many areas of European Russia and Siberia, peasants were in the habit of offering hospitality to vagrants, especially escaped convicts, for fear that otherwise their houses might be set on fire. In eastern Russia especially, where many felons were always on the run, there was the ever-present danger of a robber band taking revenge on a village that refused to harbor a fugitive member of the band or turned him over to the authorities.

The third motive for protecting the poor was more elevated. However much a robber disregarded human law, he was still conscious of his transgressions against the law of God. In many accounts of major criminals we find ascribed to them, perhaps with some exaggeration, a lively awareness of the need to expiate their sins. It is not strange, therefore, that a hand that had taken human life should afterward be opened in generosity.

The type of brigand affectionately remembered by the Russian people even today is exemplified by Emelyan Pugachev, the eighteenth-century Cossack rebel whose ferocity, generosity, and loyalty to his comrades were immortalized in Alexander Pushkin's *History of the Pugachev Revolt*, or Stenka Razin, the hero of a well-known ballad, who threw his bride, a Persian princess, into the Volga ("as a present from a Don Cossack") because his men accused him of neglecting them for a woman. These two famous rebels are glorified not only in popular memory but also by official Soviet historiography, which praises them as national heroes and liberators.*

A less-well-known brigand, Bykov, who is mentioned by Maximov, was the leader of a band in Siberia. Along with cruelty he displayed a degree of scientific curiosity unusual in one of his profession: he ordered one of his followers to disembowel a pregnant woman and explained at his trial that he wanted to see what position the fetus occupied in the womb.† Bykov also practiced the traditional Russian

---

* Paul Avrich's book *Russian Rebels 1600–1800* (New York: Schocken Books, 1972) tells the story of the Pugachev and Razin rebellions.

† The explanation may not have been truthful. In 1897, Levenstim ("Superstition and Criminal Law") observed that there were many cases of pregnant women being ripped open because of the superstition that eating the heart of an unborn baby conferred supernatural strength, and anyone who ate nine of them could commit crimes with impunity. Nevertheless, curiosity as a motive cannot be excluded. In the late 1950s, in Moscow, some vocational school pupils got hold of a woman nearing her time and jumped up and down on her belly to induce labor because, they claimed afterward to the court, they wanted to see the birth process.

form of execution: he bent two trees, tied one of the convicted man's feet to each and released them, thereby dismembering the victim.

Among his interesting notes on convicts and vagrants, Maximov observes that "the people, deluded by false idealism, fail to see the brigand as a savage, abandoned character, stained by all manner of vices and depraved to the depths of his soul." I doubt, however, that those who extolled robbers either forgot or cared how cruel they were. As will be clear from my later discussion of peasant lynch law, cruelty was not likely to arouse either astonishment or blame among the peasantry. Indeed, robbers often showed less ingenuity in torturing their victims than a peasant kangaroo court.

Traditional Russian attitudes toward the individual and toward human life were in some respects as pragmatic as the attitude toward property, although human life was protected by the precepts of religion and, it would seem, by a biological horror of murder. Just as the popular mind distinguished between one's own property (individual or collective) and others', so it drew a more or less clear line between people who belonged, whom it was a sin to kill or harm, and outsiders. Freaks of nature, accomplices of the devil, witches and wizards, and any who willfully injured the community by habitual theft or arson were relegated to the outsider class even if they were originally part of the community. As for strangers in the peasants' midst, they were generally looked on with contempt and suspicion and were, more often than not, assumed to be evil. This applied especially to neighbors of a different race in areas colonized by Russians. There were frequent collisions between the colonizers and the indigenous population, and each had equal reason to distrust the other. In cases where the non-Russians were the newcomers, it was of course even harder for them to escape being regarded as evil: one need mention only the Jews, who were actively persecuted and accused of all kinds of wrongdoings.

Members of sects outside the Orthodox Church often suffered at the hands of villagers. Yakushkin has described the beating up of converts to Stundism (an evangelical Protestant sect)[8] by an Orthodox village, and another occasion when members of the Khlysti (a schismatic sect of the Orthodox Church) were summoned to a village assembly and cruelly beaten, while a girl reputed to be a "Blessed Virgin" of the sect was stripped naked and beaten.[9]

Newcomers with no special peculiarities were not necessarily persecuted. Russia was always full of wanderers, including not only tramps but beggars, pilgrims, and itinerant merchants and craftsmen. It was traditional to offer hospitality to such people, but woe betide them if there should then be a case of arson, plague, or other misfortune: popular suspicion might well alight on the stranger, and he would pay a severe penalty. If there was a disaster involving many people, the crowd would show no mercy in its hunt for the guilty, and due process of law would be thrown to the winds.

Lynch law was prevalent for centuries in the Russian countryside and took many lives, both innocent and guilty. The picture of collective savagery that emerges from the records is hard to reconcile with the idyllic accounts of the Russian peasantry by writers who sympathized with their poverty and defended them against oppression but completely ignored their negative traits, which are of considerable significance in any analysis of Russian society past or present.*

---

* My descriptions of lynchings are taken from peasant life, since the peasantry comprised the bulk of the population. City workers were by no means averse to mob law either, but their communities were more open and the authorities closer at hand, so that lynchings were less frequent and less violent in form.

Accurate figures on lynchings are difficult to find because many cases were never discovered by the authorities; the victims were often strangers whom nobody knew or inquired about, and the rural officials usually sympathized with the crowd and turned a blind eye to the atrocities instead of reporting them. Nevertheless, all the evidence suggests that lynchings were a common occurrence. In 1884 a district medical officer in Tobolsk province performed autopsies on about two hundred corpses of people who had been lynched;[10] the population of this district in 1891 was about 250,000.[11]

Generally the whole community, or most of it, took part in the lynching, and at the outset the lynchers were sober. Sometimes they would pause to drink as the proceedings went on, and in one case a horse thief who was being beaten asked for his share. They gave him a drink ("He may be a thief, but he's a Christian, after all") and then completed the punishment by beating him to death.

Horse thieves and arsonists got the worst treatment. The ingenuity which went into their punishments is amazing, but we do not know over how many centuries they were perfected. Here are some examples:

A horse thief was stripped naked and thrown on the ground; the skin was pulled off his arms and legs, and the sinews torn out; then his head was smashed with an ax.[12]

A jagged stick was thrust into a thief's anus in such a way that it could not be pulled out again.[13]

Arsonists were pierced with nails, had their fingers broken and their sinews torn out; a Jew had his eyes gouged out as well.[14]

Some horse thieves were stripped naked in midwinter and beaten (five hundred strokes); the next day the beating was repeated, after which the peasants tied their hands together, slung them on a stick and hanged them from a tree.[15] In the eastern provinces it was common practice to tie a horse thief to a horse's tail and then drive the animal onto the steppe. In one case,[16] a peasant tied a string around a horse thief's head, inserted a stick and twisted it so that the string bit deeper and deeper. Blood gushed from the man's eyes, and eventually there was a crack—his skull had broken. "That'll teach you to steal horses!" the peasant cried.

Other methods were less imaginative: the thief was drowned in a bog, or in winter stripped and drenched with cold water until he died. The "fisherman's punishment" was often used: two holes were cut in the river ice, about ten paces apart, and the thief was dragged under water from one to the other and back again.

The punishment was not always lethal. In cases of non-serious theft,* according to Maximov,[17] a thief who had not confessed his crime would have his cap knocked off in the market, or be paraded around wearing garments that he had stolen. A woman would be stripped of her kerchief and might be led about naked or with her skirts tucked up.[18]

These summary punishments were applied not only to people caught in the act or whose guilt was well established, but also to those under suspicion of theft. For instance:

A suspect would be summoned to the village assembly and beaten; his hands would be bound with ropes and a stick inserted between them and twisted; tallow was then melted in the fire, and his buttocks were burned with it.[19]

In 1882, to extract a confession from a suspected thief, he was hung from a beam by means of twine attached to his thumbs and big toes. The soles of his feet and his calves were burned with a red-hot poker, and he was beaten on the buttocks with the head of an ax.[20]

Two men suspected of trying to steal horses were strung

---

* Besides horse stealing, the peasants punished most severely thefts of cattle, farm implements or honey—a clever thief could raid another man's hives and get his own bees to carry off the honey.

up by their big toes from a beam, and a large straw fire was lighted under them, causing severe burns. They were then turned over to the authorities.[21]

Mob law was also used to enforce community rules— e.g., that women must not start to weave linen until all the men had left for the fields to plow, or that one must not eat while mending the fence around the cattle pasture (otherwise bears would eat the cattle)[22]—but the punishment for violating such taboos was comparatively mild.

There were stern penalties for unchaste behavior: a woman might be stripped, smeared with tar and chased about the village with loud cries, or two adulterers might be stripped, bound together, and chased in the same way. In some places the husband of an adulterous wife was expected to tie her to the shaft of a cart, harness horses to it, and drive about the village while he lashed the unfortunate woman with his whip.

There were savage lynchings of people suspected of sorcery or of casting the evil eye. Historians of popular customs sometimes overlook the fact that Russian peasants lived in permanent terror of witchcraft and were constantly hunting out its supposed practitioners in order to render them harmless. It was not necessary to be a soothsayer or to claim supernatural powers to be suspected of being in league with the devil, although this kind of boasting was quite common. Suspicion might fall on any villager, especially if he or she was distinguished from birth by some physical mark ("the devil's sign") or if something happened that seemed clearly due to the devil's agency. Extreme old age was also a sign of diabolical protection, and aged crones were as much feared as if they had really been witches. A calamity like a drought or a cattle plague drew popular wrath on a "witch" or "wizard," who was forthwith punished without mercy. Sometimes, while it was clear that a witch had been at work, it was not certain who she was.

In that case, as in medieval Europe, the accusers resorted to trial by water. The suspects were thrown into a lake or river, and the one who did not sink was a witch.[23] Levenstim published a description of this procedure in 1897:

> The woman's hands were bound and a stone tied round her neck; if she sank, she generally drowned, as help was slow in coming, but if she failed to sink she was burned as a witch. This mode of investigation illustrates the helplessness of a woman accused of witchcraft. Unfortunately this old superstition is still prevalent in all parts of Russia, with only a slight change: the peasants now believe that this procedure is also a sure remedy for drought.

The same author goes on:

> In 1875 the peasants of a village in western Russia wished to find out which of their womenfolk was a witch and asked the landowner if they might use his pond for the purpose; when he refused, they got a midwife to examine the women to see if any of them had a tail.

Levenstim also notes that accusations of sorcery or witchcraft were used to settle private accounts, even between members of the same family. Here is his account of an incident that took place in Moscow:

> Cases of crude and bestial violence inspired by a belief in witchcraft occur not only in the depths of the country but even in large cities, among whose populations there are many superstitious people. As evidence of this sad truth, let me cite an incident that occurred in the very center of Moscow, on Nikolskaya Street, near the shrine of St. Panteleimon, which is always surrounded by a crowd of sick people. Early in the morning of September 25, 1895, there was in the crowd a boy named Vasily Alekseyev who was subject

to fits. A peasant woman, Natalia Novikova, talked to the boy and gave him an apple; he bit into it and suddenly had a fit of hysterics. Hearing his cries, a constable rushed up from the nearby police station and took him there to recover. But the crowd was not satisfied with this. Believing that Novikova was a witch and had cast a spell on the apple, they seized her and beat her half to death.

Village courts, too, were fearful of magic spells. Levenstim has still another account:

In 1886 the Talyansk village court in the Umansk district of Kiev province was trying a case between two peasants, B. and K. The latter told the court that his adversary was practicing witchcraft to secure a decision in his favor. At K.'s request, B. was searched and was found to have in his cap a few bits of rag, a piece of string, and some herbs. The court decided that these were magic charms, and instead of trying the original action, sentenced B. to twenty strokes of the birch.

On one occasion, in a case of assault involving two women, a village court noticed that one of them was scattering poppy seeds around the bench; this was deemed to be sorcery, and she was fined 3 rubles.[24]

Although the examples given here are drawn from peasant life at the end of the past century, it would be naïve to suppose that traditions and beliefs of such long standing have been eradicated by the social transformations that have taken place since. Many things, of course, have changed, and many traditional practices now appear in new and unexpected forms, but although modern observers tend to ignore them, there are traces of the old attitudes in the criminal tradition of present-day Russia.

The transformation of the Russian criminal tradition into a specifically Soviet one is the subject of the next chapter. I will conclude here by considering a phenomenon that is as common today as it ever was—the violent brawls that break out on feast days and holidays. These occur all over Russia, but unfortunately they have been little studied. In their published reports, Soviet investigators do not probe the origins of these incidents in the countryside; they generally confine themselves to observing that drunkenness leads to hooliganism, that there is more drunkenness in the countryside during religious holidays, and that the solution is to step up atheist propaganda in the rural areas. All the evidence suggests, however, that these drunken brawls are rooted in ancient customs and longstanding social antagonisms.

In the 1920s, criminologist T. Segalov[25] tried to interest his confreres in the subject. Searching for the causes of the outbursts, he observed: "Brawls at weddings, christenings and wakes are essentially quarrels over seniority, honor, and social position, and in many ways resemble the quarrels of precedence among the boyars of old Russia—they stem from matters of 'place' or social rank."

He also found the following:

> A frequent cause of a free-for-all in which heads are broken and bellies slashed with knives is the arrival in a village of a band of roistering youths accompanied by an accordion player, who swagger about and make up to the local girls. The resentment this arouses is general; there is no indication that a young man from one village is jealous of one of the outsiders because of a particular girl. Individual cases of sexual jealousy leading to murder and mayhem are different in nature and much rarer than drunken brawls resulting from collective jealousy. The complaint is usually along these lines: "They came to play around in our village, with our girls, and we were angry with them because they had beaten up our people in the past." It is interesting that in factories located in rural areas, where the workman who runs a machine today may have been at

the plow yesterday—and may be back at the plow
tomorrow—the outbreaks of collective hooliganism
appear to have similar motivations, and the old country concept "Don't come near our road" is broadened
to include "our barracks" or "our entry."

Segalov did not overlook the role that fear of magic
played in starting brawls:

From reports of brawls in which people were killed
for eating a sausage too many in a strange place or
grabbing an empty glass off a table set for guests and
refusing to give it back, it can be clearly seen that the
real object of the quarrel was not the glass or the
sausage but a distorted survival of ancient local or
class rivalries that have degenerated over the course
of centuries. Survivals of serfdom and of the feudal
period when our frontiers were expanded by conquest
have poisoned social relations in the countryside in the
same way that memories of Paganism and Christianity
have distorted the people's attitudes toward nature and
the environment. As Yesenin wrote: "Unclean forces
have so frightened us that we scent witchcraft every
time we see a hole in the ice." In the law courts we see
this side of country life mainly in the prosecutions
undertaken under Article 174 of the Criminal Code
[which deals with false accusations of sorcery]; but
anyone who has ever observed the behavior of young
people, elders, guests and their kinfolk at a village
wedding is aware of the atmosphere of tension and
fear lest some open or, more likely, covert manifestation of witchcraft appear.*

Segalov unfortunately failed to persuade Soviet research-
ers to focus on this problem, and later official publications
give the impression that the psychology of the countryside

---

* The fear has diminished today, but it is reasonable to suppose that
traces of it still remain.

changed so rapidly and so completely that the motives Segalov discussed are no longer pertinent. Drunken brawls continue, however, and their deep-seated causes are still not clear. They can hardly be due altogether to new types of social antagonism arising from "socialist competition," although this may play a part in some cases. Here is a modern instance of a brawl at a wedding: Citizen S. picked a quarrel with members of a wedding party who refused him a glass of vodka, and inflicted severe injuries on one of them. The Supreme Court of the Byelorussian SSR confirmed his conviction on charges of "grievous bodily harm and hooliganism."[26]

2
The Soviet Criminal Tradition

In discussing the Soviet criminal tradition separately, I do not mean to imply that it has completely superseded the older Russian tradition. On the contrary, many features of that older tradition persist in the Soviet Union. But the new regime has so altered morals and manners that a distinct Soviet criminal tradition has already emerged.

Here, as almost everywhere in this book, I am referring to "Russia" in the narrow sense, excluding non-Russian nationalities but including areas colonized by Russians or those whose native populations have been expelled and largely replaced by Russians. Russians comprise about 50 percent of the population of the Soviet Union. There are fifteen Union Republics in the USSR, the largest of which is the Russian Soviet Federated Socialist Republic (RSFSR, or Russian Republic). In addition to the substantial Russian majority, the RSFSR contains so many Ukrainians, Jews, Yakuts, and Ossetins that parts of it have been subdivided into "Autonomous Republics" named after the predominant minority group, e.g., the Buryat (Mongol) Autonomous Republic. This book is primarily concerned with crime in the Russian regions of the RSFSR; where reference is made to non-Russian customs or incidents, it is always specified. Each Union Republic has its own Criminal Code; all Codes are similar but the numbering of Articles differs from Republic to Republic. Unless otherwise indicated, reference to Articles of the Criminal Code refer to the Criminal Code of the RSFSR.

A study of the Soviet criminal tradition should properly begin at the turn of the present century when the first preparations for a new order in Russia were being made. In fact, the Russian tradition of regarding brigands as liberators of the people played an important part in those preparations. To be sure, the early revolutionaries differed from the brigands of old, who appeared first as robbers and then as liberators, in both popular estimation and their own. The revolutionaries began by regarding themselves as liberators and resorted to pillage and terror only as a means of raising funds for their cause. At the same time they encouraged sections of the community to rob and destroy in order to sow confusion and expedite the process of "liberation." Of all the major revolutionary parties, the Bolsheviks were the most active in stirring up the population by any available method and inciting mob violence as a means of destroying the old regime.

The Bolshevik leaders were not all of one mind about pillage and violence (so-called partisan activities), but on the whole they energetically supported them. They definitely, for example, helped to organize the riots of 1905, although their present claims about their role seem to be exaggerated.* To obtain funds, both the Social Revolutionaries and the Bolsheviks were active in organizing armed robberies, which were euphemistically known as

---

* These riots were often mentioned in official reports on crime in later years. In 1917 in an article on "Fluctuations of Criminality," A. Melnikov observed: "The acts of expropriation by violence which began under the banner of the political struggle were bound to degenerate almost immediately into criminal acts without a shred of political justification."[1]

"expropriations." (The abbreviation for "expropriations" was "exes," and this expression has now become part of Russian thieves' slang.[2]) And many among the liberal intelligentsia at the beginning of this century not only did not condemn such revolutionary crimes but actually seemed to admire them.

Until the Revolution, the Bolsheviks freely admitted that they stole to keep the Party going. Lenin publicly declared that the Bolsheviks, as he put it, "stole what had been stolen," and he himself helped to organize systematic robberies to provide funds for the Party and the Revolution. Such robberies were apparently widespread; the best-known of their perpetrators was a thief named Semyon Ter-Petrosyan (1882–1922), an Armenian Bolshevik, who used the pseudonym Kamo. Kamo's bold operations were carried out under Stalin's direction. His most famous exploit, robbing the post-office coach on Erevan Square in Tbilisi (Tiflis) in 1907, seems to have helped the Bolsheviks' prestige more than their treasury—it is said that the Party never succeeded in spending the stolen rubles. Indeed, the future Soviet ministers Maxim Litvinov and Nikolai Semashko were arrested when they tried to exchange them for foreign currency.[3]

When the Bolsheviks came to power, they realized that their international prestige demanded that the memory of their expropriations be allowed to fade. Soviet publications, therefore, have little or nothing to say about this aspect of partisan warfare. Stalin always preferred not to publicize his part in it, and Kamo died in mysterious circumstances soon after the Revolution. On that occasion the newspaper *Zarya Vostoka* (Eastern Dawn) reported:

> By an evil trick of fate, Kamo met his death on the streets of Tbilisi just as his comrades had persuaded him to write his memoirs . . . and had found him secretaries to assist him. Comrade Kamo is dead, and with

him died the possibility of compiling an account of our Party's past activity in Transcaucasia.

It was not only in Transcaucasia, however, that expropriations had taken place. On July 18, 1922, after Kamo's death, the Georgian Bolshevik Philip Makharadze wrote in *Zarya Vostoka*: "Expropriations were not haphazard, there was a system and a far-reaching plan. The plan embraced all Russia, and its presiding genius . . . was Kamo."

In a eulogy at Kamo's funeral Sergo Ordzhonikidze, Stalin's lieutenant in the Caucasus and later Commissar of Heavy Industry, declared: "More than once you expounded your plans for the fight against capitalism. Sometimes they appeared to be impractical fantasies. . . . I remember how you used to talk about them to Comrade Lenin, the leader of the Revolution, who loved you like a brother."

In the post-Stalin era, Kamo's achievements became the subject of a film entitled *Personally Known*, which included sequences on the Tbilisi robbery. There was one curious detail. In Soviet eyes, every aspect of a criminal trial has a class bias, including the testimony of expert witnesses, yet in the film a German bourgeois psychiatrist sees through Kamo's feigned madness but abandons his own class and his professional scruples to give a false diagnosis that will save the thief and the Party from criminal proceedings. For this he receives the thanks of the German Social-Democrat Karl Liebknecht. The episode appears to be pure invention.

As is well known, the "liberators" of Russia not only robbed but also killed, first as terrorists and partisans, and afterward as rulers. The number of lives they took has been discussed by many writers, and I will not go into it here. But in accordance with the old Russian tradition, the terrorists and "expropriators" appear as heroes and liberators, not only in official propaganda but in popular legend as well.

Once they had gained power, the Bolshevik liberators did

not abandon the principle that the end justifies the means. On the contrary, they applied it more widely than ever, especially to property, making full use of the national tradition that other people's property is fair game. They declared that in the future all property of any magnitude would be held in common, and they incited the proletariat to pillage. In the name of the State they plundered churches and took over private possessions. In the course of time the proletariat came to realize that communal ownership meant simply that property, instead of belonging to an individual, now belonged to a superproprietor, the State; but initially they believed that they were seizing property in order to make it their own, although it was to be held in common and not individually.

After the Revolution it appeared that the ancient dream of plundering the rich to feed the hungry had been realized, and it was nobody's fault that feeding the hungry proved more difficult than anticipated. New problems arose, and it rapidly became clear that even though the wealthy had disappeared, the hungry would have to feed themselves by their own efforts.

Bolshevik decrees sanctioned theft on a national scale. Since the Bolsheviks had won the day and founded a new state that was accorded recognition by traditional states, it appeared to follow that the expropriations were legitimate. There are many examples in history of a conqueror's acts being legalized in this way, although from the point of view of judicial and even revolutionary tradition they might seem to have no more legal force than, say, the decrees issued by the outlaw Pugachev. It is especially difficult to claim legitimacy for the seizure of state power by the Bolsheviks, who had forcibly dispersed the popularly elected Constituent Assembly. The Assembly first met on January 18, 1918. Two days earlier, the Central Executive Committee of the Party had adopted a decree stating that any attempt to assume the functions of State power should be regarded as counterrevolutionary. The Constituent Assembly, which claimed to exercise State authority, fell under this ban, and on January 19 the Executive Committee issued a decree dissolving it.

What the Bolsheviks really objected to was not that the Assembly would determine the form of government of postrevolutionary Russia, but that their Party was in a minority in it. Although almost all the voters were workers or peasants and most of them did not vote for the Bolsheviks, we are informed by a recent Soviet history book[4] that "the working masses of Russia unanimously approved of the liquidation of the Assembly."

I have written elsewhere[5] that I recognize the existing authority in the USSR *de jure*, yet I have just said that Soviet power was based on brigandage. Where does one draw the line between usurpers and lawful rulers? This is too hard a question for me and, I believe, for others as well: it has arisen many times in history and has always puzzled those who have tried to think in terms of law. So, without discussing whether the Bolsheviks in the late 1920s were usurpers or lawful rulers, let us consider how they made use of the Russian criminal tradition in order to liquidate the kulaks.

The existence of successful farmers with property of their own did not suit the Soviet authorities, whose support among the peasantry was confined to its proletarianized members. Well-to-do peasants, or kulaks ("fists") as they were abusively called, were a vexation because of the Soviet doctrine requiring the liquidation of private ownership of the means of production. Moreover, the kulaks were respected by other peasants for their experience (which greatly surpassed that of the average collective farm manager) and as employers, since they paid better wages and set an example of hard work that put the collective farms to shame.

The regime could not afford to make peace with the

kulaks, since this would have meant postponing the political subjugation of the bulk of the population and the consolidation of Bolshevik power. It was tactically risky, however, to liquidate them from above, using the State's authority and punitive apparatus, because of their prestige in the countryside and because the peasantry's ancient ideas of community solidarity had not yet been wholly eradicated. Hence the regime resorted to propaganda and "permitted" the peasantry, or rather peasant organizations, to abolish the kulaks as a class, i.e., to take away their property and give it to the collective farms while the kulaks themselves and their families were deported by government decree. Enough volunteers were found among the poorest peasants to carry out these measures—the kulaks had been declared aliens, and the dispossession of aliens is an old Russian tradition.

There is evidence that in many areas the liquidation of the kulaks led to peasant uprisings,* but there is no reason to think that these uprisings were in defense of the kulaks. The liquidation was accompanied by "overzealous measures" of collectivization, and all the signs are that the peasants were revolting in defense of their own property. How prominent ex-kulaks were in the uprisings is hard to say. Much has been written about their desperate resis-

---

* Soviet historians are generally silent about these. That the years of collectivization were a challenge to the fighting efficiency of the Red Army is clear from Commissar of Defense Kliment Voroshilov's speech at the Sixteenth Congress of the All-Union Communist Party in 1930: "Difficulties with grain procurement, the activities of kulak elements, overzealous measures connected with collectivization in some places, pressure from the petty bourgeoisie, and the intrigues of right-wing deviationists—all these, Comrades, were factors which gave us plenty of opportunity to test to the full the political steadfastness of the Red Army masses and their devotion to the cause of the Revolution. Having put them to the test we can say with pride that despite all difficulties and despite the intensification of the class struggle during these two and a half years, the Red Army did not flinch."[6]

tance, and the kulak attacking peasant activists with a sawed-off shotgun is a stock figure in official Soviet histories. A farmer reduced to despair may indeed resort to such weapons, but it is uncertain how far the kulaks were able to offer serious resistance. In any case, they met with no sympathy from the authorities, who took from them all they had. Pity for the kulaks was in fact condemned on ideological grounds. Thus a Party member named Korshon at the Sixteenth Party Congress[7] denounced the "class-ridden" attitude of a Professor Shirenko who had pointed out that "the kulaks are dying of hunger, and to 'liquidate' them is simply to finish off starving people who have long since ceased to be kulaks and are poorer than the poorest."

There is a well-known instance in which the Soviet authorities pandered to the Russian people's traditional attitude toward others' property. During the closing phase of World War II, the officers and men of the Red Army were allowed to "expropriate" civilian property on conquered bourgeois territory.* Soviet warriors and their families seem to have felt no qualms about this application of the spoils system to the nation's enemies. It need hardly be said that German plundering and excesses on Soviet territory were not a sufficient justification for similar acts on the part of the Red Army; retaliation of this kind is scarcely compatible with the principles of international law.

Expropriations of this kind were indeed defined as "pillage" in the Criminal Code of 1922,[8] but the 1927 Soviet decree on military crimes[9] restricts the term "pillage" to spoils taken from the killed and wounded on the field of battle, while plundering the population of the battle area falls under a different article. I do not know how often this article was applied in practice to expropriations of this sort, or how organized such expropriations were. A friend who

---

* The official arrangements made to send this booty back to the USSR are described in Lev Koplev's book *To Be Preserved Forever.*

was an intelligence officer at the front and is now employed
in a research institute told me the following story. "We were
told to pull in a prisoner for questioning. We did so and, of
course, began by searching him. My fellow officer took a
handsome pipe off the man, and I took a great big watch, a
gold one with a chain. On the way to the commanding
officer we ran into our lieutenant, who said, 'Listen, you
don't need that watch, give it to me.' I wasn't pleased, but I
gave it to him, of course. He walked off a couple of hundred
yards, and bang! a shell dropped right where he was standing. Since then I haven't taken a watch from anyone!"

The traditional attitude toward other people's property
was first exploited by the authorities for the purpose of the
class struggle, and one might say that thanks to their encouragement, it spread to a much larger portion of the population than ever before. Nowadays, however, it has turned
against the authorities themselves. Even the proletariat soon
realized that nationalized property was not, in fact, common property. With all its propaganda, the new regime did
not succeed in persuading people to protect state property
as their own; they continued to regard it as someone else's
and treated it accordingly. This seems to be true today of
the entire population; everyone steals a bit here and there.
There is even a saying that the only man who doesn't steal
is the man who has no opportunity.

To be sure, the attitude toward State property is no new
thing in Russia. I have already mentioned illegal woodcut-
ting and similar depredations. Nicholas I is said to have told
his son and heir during the Crimean War: "I believe you
and I are the only people in Russia who don't steal."[10]
Conditions today seem to be similar, but infinitely worse. I
shall return to this later but might mention here that at the
present time very mild punishments are imposed for petty
thefts of state property. Under Stalin the penalties were extremely harsh, even in the case of hungry people stealing

scraps of food from the State. This severity swelled the population of the prison camps but did not prevent theft; in all probability the national tradition is too strong to be quelled by any amount of repression.

The authorities were more successful in coping with the national tradition of mob violence.* It was prohibited by law, since, in the words of the Supreme Court of the USSR,[11] "even in so-called spontaneous instances of private justice, the guiding hand of the class enemy is often discernible." Mob law was punished as a major infringement of public order, for which the organizers—and it was always possible to "identify" organizers of popular outbreaks—were liable to penalties up to and including execution (Article 59 of the 1926 Criminal Code).† Nevertheless, the victory over mob rule in its earlier forms appears to have been the result not of legal prohibition but of two other causes.

First, the new regime abolished the peasant commune, which in former times protected its members and punished

* This, however, applies only to the period, after mob violence ceased to be exploited in the class struggle. There is abundant evidence that immediately before and after the seizure of power, the Bolsheviks, taking advantage of the population's natural propensities, incited peasants to burn and pillage landowners' estates and kulak farms.

† Here is an example of the exploitation of mob law by the class enemy: In January 1934, in the "New World" kolkhoz (collective farm) at Lebezhinsky village in the Isil-Kulsk district of western Siberia, in a camp where the work teams that had done the threshing were stationed, farm personnel of both sexes who were absent or turned up late for work were beaten with wooden spoons, in public, on the lower parts of the body. In the course of a month, thirteen persons were beaten in this way, including eleven women, one of whom was over four months pregnant. The proceedings imitated those of a formal court, with a judge, prosecuting and defending attorneys, clerks, and so on. The instigator and organizer was a member of one of the teams named Bazhenkov, who belonged to the kulak class and whose father had been deported during the collectivization in 1930. (A. Shlyapochnikov in *Problems of Criminal Policy*, Vol. I, Moscow, 1935).

wrongdoers. It may seem strange that the Soviets, who introduced collectivization, at the same time destroyed the communal system bequeathed them by history; but they had to do so. The village commune resisted external control and had to be replaced by a collective organization amenable to State authority. The links between members of the new collective were, of course, nothing like as strong as those between members of the previous commune, and so far as I can judge, the collective did not practice the system of mutual responsibility so characteristic of the commune. Hence it hardly ever happened on a collective farm, as it did in the commune, that the peasants prevented a serious crime from coming to the notice of the authorities.

Second, the Soviet regime turned the instinct of private vengeance into another channel and made it much easier to satisfy. Whereas in the past it was necessary to secure the unanimity of a crowd to avenge a wrong, between 1920 and 1950 an aggrieved individual had only to denounce his neighbor to the authorities as a kulak, a kulak's henchman, a spy, a diversionist, etc., and the State would take care of the rest; as often as not the person informed against would disappear never to return.

How much terror was required before people who used to despise informers became accustomed to betraying their neighbors and guarding against betrayal by them is a question that awaits the attention of Soviet psychologists. At all events, there is much evidence that in former times the peasants found it repugnant to inform on one another. For example, the ethnographer Prince V. V. Tenishchev remarked that in the nineteenth century "the obligation to inform the authorities of the commission of a crime is by no means taken for granted, and the peasants take an unfavorable view of denunciation." There are many Russian proverbs reflecting a preference for minding one's own business —"I live outside the village, it's not my affair"—and many derogatory terms for the informer—busybody, blabbermouth, devil's lawyer, and so on.

It is true that informers are not popular in Soviet times either, and ordinary peasants who write secret reports to the authorities are liable to have an unpleasant time if their fellows find them out.* But the official view is that the distrust of informers is another manifestation of the hidden hand of the class enemy.

Happily, secret denunciations are not so common now as they were from 1920 to 1950. Instead, meetings are organized at which members of the collective are rebuked for misbehavior, unchastity, drunkenness or dangerous thoughts. These meetings can be quite violent affairs, but on the whole the instinct for mob law has been tamed and expresses itself more decorously than it used to. Physical violence has not disappeared, of course, and what looks like an ordinary fight may well contain an element of private justice, individual or collective, but such instances are fewer and less ferocious than they once were.

Advocates of mob law and unofficial justice are found not only among workers and peasants. A research worker told me that thefts of radio spare parts were common in his establishment, and that military research centers have an excellent system of stopping them. He had seen a soldier in a laboratory stop a junior technician, feel his pockets, pull out a spare part and "give him a crack on the jaw that sent him right across the room." My informant, an intellectual, evidently thought this a first-class method.

Alexander Solzhenitsyn has also expressed regret in *The Gulag Archipelago* (Vol. 2, p. 432) that people no longer take justice into their own hands. He writes: "Any genuine

---

* The government organized a network of "worker-peasant correspondents" to keep the authorities informed about local events and the mood of the populace. These correspondents were distrusted by their co-workers and there are many reports of reprisals against them.

initiative like that shown in the French film *Quai des brumes*, in which the workers went about catching thieves and punishing them themselves without the knowledge of the authorities would, in our country, have been suppressed as illicit! Could one even *imagine* that way of thinking and that sort of film in our country?"

3

The Professional Underworld

Soviet criminologists insist that the USSR, unlike Western countries, has no such thing as organized crime. This is true in the sense that differences exist between the Russian underworld and what we generally call an organization. It is likely, however, that what Soviet experts have in mind is not the precise differences between Western and Soviet criminal gangs, but the fact that organized extortion of protection money from the public is not practiced in Russia. This indeed appears to be the case, although there were signs of such a practice in the last century: peasants would pay an agreed sum of money to a harborer of thieves, who in return promised that their horses would not be stolen. Such agreements were even registered with the village authorities.[1] Apparently this form of insurance has not survived in present-day Russia.

Soviet propaganda is even more emphatic as to the non-existence of a Soviet underworld. Everyone in Russia is aware that the underworld continues to exist and that its leaders are called bosses (*pakhany*) or regulars (*vory v zakone*), but a very different story is told in an interview in the *Literary Gazette* with a lieutenant who is an educational officer in one of the forced labor camps:

33

Journalist: "Bosses and regulars, do they still exist, or is that all a thing of the past?"

Lieutenant: "Not a sign of it any more. It didn't exist when I was first assigned to the job—I only read about it in Lev Sheinin's books."[2]*

The idea that the criminal world no longer exists is also attested in the *Literary Gazette* of April 3, 1974, by a former member of it, Alexei Frolov, who is now a master craftsman in a technical college. He writes:

> There is no longer such a thing as a criminal underworld; it was destroyed. I am not referring, of course, to criminality in general, but to that organized, self-contained, antisociety that did not even recognize the fatherland—"A thief's country is any place where he can steal." That world no longer exists. As for the individuals or groups of two or three who commit crimes nowadays, sooner or later they end up in jail or in a hard-labor colony, and things there are not the same as they were twenty-five years ago.
>
> The underworld itself is a thing of the past, but I hear clear echoes of it from time to time. . . . There is no underworld, but its ghost still haunts a number of people, and it is real enough to them!

But despite such official claims, the underworld has survived to this day, especially that sector of it known as the thieves' world (*vorovskoy mir*), which deserves to be regarded as a social institution since it has its own internal cohesion and ethical code.

Ordinary criminals, of whom there are plenty in Russia, may commit illegal acts either occasionally or systematically, but they remain members of the society and profess more or less the same ethics as the rest of the population. Members of the thieves' world, on the other hand, are only

---

* Lev Sheinin is the author of *Zapiski sledovatelya* (Notes of a Criminal Investigator), Moscow, 1968.

externally members of society; the ethics of their own sub-group require them to divorce themselves from it and to reject all ordinary social ties, such as family relationships and obligations of all kinds.

It is significant that the members of this particular underworld are thieves, i.e., people who reject the right of ownership as a social institution. But not every thief belongs to the thieves' world, which rejects other institutions as well as property.

The closed and exotic character of the thieves' world and the ability of its members to live detached from society make it attractive to other criminals who have not rejected all social ties. They often imitate it or claim to belong to it when they do not. This makes it extremely difficult to study. Its would-be denizens offer misleading accounts, while its real members so appreciate its unique and esoteric character that they are most unlikely to write memoirs or otherwise enlighten observers about its nature and activities.

There was a period in the recent history of Russia when many educated observers appeared to have an opportunity to make direct contact with the underworld leaders. During those same years of 1920 to 1950, political prisoners were put in labor camps with criminals of all kinds, and quite a number of the "politicals" were competent social investigators. But many factors, including the high mortality rate, prevented their talents from being properly put to use—who knows how many sociological studies perished in the camps with their authors? Beyond that, the criminals and their potential investigators did not, as a rule, meet on the right footing: the former persecuted their political fellow inmates so mercilessly that unprejudiced contact was impossible. Nonetheless, accounts of camp life by former political prisoners sometimes contain valuable, dispassionate information about the criminal world. One of the most important of these writers is Varlam Shalamov, whose medical duties in the camps brought him into contact with many criminals and who, while he was horrified by what he saw, was able to record his observations with a certain amount of objectivity.*

Many writers of fiction, fascinated by the romance and exoticism of the underworld, have used it as a setting and endowed their criminal characters with attractive or repulsive qualities according to their taste. But it is easy to see that their sources of information are confined to the small fry of underworld society or to spurious members of it. An exception is *The Thieves' Dens of St. Petersburg*, by V. V. Krestovsky (1840–95).[3] Krestovsky's knowledge of thieves' cant appears authentic if now somewhat dated, and the book is full of interest, although it describes a motley cross-section of the criminal world at a level considerably below that of the big bosses.

It is quite possible that the archives of Soviet public prosecutors and the KGB (Committee of State Security) contain valuable information on this subject. There is no lack of investigators and sources of information in such circles, and it is known that quite important figures in the criminal world have from time to time broken down and told authorities all they knew. How far such information is made available to Soviet scholars is anyone's guess, but certainly there are no Soviet publications dealing with the structure and customs of the underworld. This may, however, be due to the vigilance of the censorship, which prevents demoralizing information from reaching the public.

Since the Russian underworld has a long history and is highly conservative in its organizational and ethical prin-

* Two brief stories by Shalamov were published in *Russia's Other Writers*, ed. Michael Scammell (New York, 1971). A collection of Shalamov's stories has been published in French: Verlam Chalamov [*sic*], *Récits de Kolyma* (Paris, 1969).

ciples, we can find out something about it by studying other analogous associations that existed in Russia in former times and evolved their own specific ethics and customs.

It should not, therefore, appear to be a digression if I now introduce a brief description of the *artel*, that ancient Russian institution which preserved its original form up to the beginning of this century and which is still not completely extinct. Around 1900 the term *artel* was used to denote a wide range of associations, generally of an economic nature, which went by different names in different parts of the country, the names sometimes denoting an artel specializing in a certain occupation. The internal organization of these bodies varied considerably. In some cases, especially in the nineteenth century, there was a written charter, and the functions of some artels were prescribed by laws dating from the eighteenth century. In the present context, however, I am concerned with those artels that functioned on the basis of oral or even tacit agreement among their members. This was the prevailing type, and there were so many of these that some late nineteenth-century authors maintained that it would be impossible to imagine Russia or the Russians without the artel system.[4] So strong was the artel spirit, indeed, that the term was used in popular speech to denote any joint effort by a number of people.

In the middle of the last century, as statute law was extended to a wider and wider range of civil relationships, the fact that the artel was based on customary law gave rise to some difficulties, and there were those who urged the government to lay down uniform regulations for the conduct of artels. Yakushin, an expert on Russian customary law,[5] observed that "if general rules were laid down for artels they would almost certainly remain a dead letter, and this would be all to the good since the variety of artels is such that they cannot be regimented." Nevertheless, the process of regimentation went forward, and in Soviet times the term was used for the pseudoindependent associations devised by the new regime, such as collective farms and groups of craftsmen, fishermen, and so on. These "artels" were not only regulated in their internal structure but were also completely subordinated to the State and Party administration. They had so little independence that it was not even possible to resign from membership. As a result of these bogus artels, the term ceased to be used in its former sense of a free association with certain rules or in the sense of a joint effort.

Nevertheless, the idea of an artel in its original sense remains alive to this day among the Russian people. Even though the state discourages any form of genuinely free association, groups devoted to various economic purposes continue to be formed on the basis of time-honored customs. The survival of the artel principle can be seen on almost any occasion when a group of workers carries out a private commission. The same workers may belong to a team (*brigada*) for their regular jobs, but outside the official framework they will form an association of their own on artel lines. So do young people when they want to go on excursions; and for the time being, private tourism is allowed to flourish, although the government—sometimes out of concern for the safety of such groups—requires prior notification of itineraries and the names of those in charge. Yet another survival of cooperative customs is the practice of joining together for holiday celebrations, which recalls the Christmas clubs formerly organized by young people in peasant communities.[6]

Although I have called the artel a typical Russian institution, other countries have had similar associations in their early history. The artel is one of the most primitive forms of economic association, and its very simplicity is the reason it has survived and adapted itself to all manner of condition and purposes.

The essence of an artel is that its members agree, orally or tacitly, to carry out some economic activity on the basis of equal rights and responsibilities. In other words, the artel is responsible for seeing that engagements agreed to by members in its name are carried out, and the members in their turn are responsible for the performance of engagements contracted by the artel. The important thing is that an obligation incurred by a representative of the artel has to be fulfilled. Members of the artel are also responsible for any damage to the artel or to the other contracting party that is caused by a fault of theirs. A member may be held responsible to the extent of his entire property except for the minimum necessary to maintain himself and his family, and if his assets are not sufficient to cover the damage, it becomes the collective responsibility of the artel.

The artel was governed by a chief or elder elected by the members. He generally had no special privileges but was responsible for the efficient management of the association and for concluding agreements and transacting business on its behalf. If he mismanaged, another election was held, and he was replaced. In some artels the position was held in rotation.

The principle of equal rights meant that members had an equal voice in decisions of common concern and were entitled to equal profits in return for a given input of labor (or labor and capital). In some cases, where it was appropriate to the artel's activity, the members clubbed together to provide food and other necessities of life. In addition to full members there were also apprentices, who received a lesser share of the profits or none at all. In some artels women received only a half share, but this was not a general rule; usually they shared equally. There were also artels, where a particular kind of work was done, composed of women only. In many cases, though not all, there were arrangements for mutual aid among members; for example, one who fell ill would be looked after and provided with food.

Members who disregarded their obligations or offended the general morality had sanctions imposed on them by the artel. Those who came to work drunk were generally fined. Another penalty was to be excluded from the artel's work, and hence from a share in the profits, for one or more days.

The principles that governed workmen's artels also applied to those of tradesmen, hawkers, and—of particular interest to our present theme—beggars. The members of beggars' artels depended on the association to a much greater extent than workers did, and in this they resembled thieves, of whom we will speak presently. Beggars' artels were characterized by a dividing-up of territory, which sometimes led to very sharp disputes: Sergei Maximov (*Fatherland Notes*, 1869) reported a case in which a group of beggars' artels joined together to exclude a rival artel from a fairground.[7] Like thieves' artels, the beggars' associations were secret and used a special language unintelligible to outsiders.

> All the beggars of this place for a considerable distance around constitute a regularly organized association known as the "beggars' guild," with an elected "guildmaster" and with its own laws, customs and language. New members are nominated by their comrades and must accept the obligations of the guild. A person entitled to practice as a beggar by reason of physical deformity or disablement is apprenticed for a time to a fellow beggar, after which he is enrolled on a list and has to pay a subscription. As a rule the term of apprenticeship is six years and the subscription is 60 kopecks (about one dollar); but an apprentice may elect to serve a shorter term and pay a higher subscription. Membership in the guild is effected by a special ceremony. The aspiring member is brought into the assembly, and after mutual greetings, the guildmaster tests his knowledge of the prayers, beggars' songs, and

special language of the fraternity. The apprentice bows and kisses the hand of each person present, and is then admitted as a member. A feast is given in his honor, and on this occasion he is allowed for the first time to sit with the others.

The guildmaster is elected for an indefinite period and is generally a blind beggar; he convokes the guild for necessary business, including the punishment of transgressors. This used to take the form of beating but is now usually a fine for the purchase of church candles. The most ignominious punishment consists of slitting the offender's wallet, signifying that he is no longer entitled to practice as a beggar. A steward is elected to look after funds and expenses. Both extraordinary and annual assemblies are held, the latter on the first Monday of Lent or on Whitsunday, when a new candle is placed in the church on behalf of the fraternity. The funds accumulated by the guild are generally devoted to church purposes. . . . The beggars have a language of their own, which they endeavor to keep secret from outsiders.[8]

Members of the artels described in this chapter were free to leave them at any time. For that reason I consider them liberal artels as opposed to the totalitarian ones now to be described. There was still one other kind of association, the prison artel, whose members belonged not by contract but by virtue of their incarceration in a given place.*

There are references to artels of thieves, including horse thieves, in Russian juridical literature from the middle of the last century onwards. Nowadays the term is seldom used, but to judge from Lev Sheinin's *Notes of a Criminal Investigator* (1968),[9] it still seems to have been in the 1920s, at the time of the New Economic Policy (NEP).

Unfortunately, I have been unable to find any literature

---

* Some description of these prison artels may be found in Dostoevsky's *House of the Dead*, and traces of artel customs still survive in prisons and labor camps.

that studies thieves' artels specifically. It is known that they differed from normal artels by virtue of their totalitarian character and the fact that a thief was not allowed to leave and return to a law-abiding life. The criminal world attaches so much importance to secrecy and to the principle of "honor among thieves" that a man who deserts the fraternity is regarded as a traitor.*

Many closed associations, to be sure, have a similar attitude, among them strict religious orders and secret political organizations, not to mention the many "voluntary" associations in present-day Russia that do not permit their members to resign. The most important of these is the Communist Party. Any member who seeks to resign is expelled on the ground of "conduct unbecoming to a Communist." Another example is the KGB. A Soviet citizen I know, who was thinking of taking a job in that organization, was told: "Of course you realize there's no resigning from our service." Indeed the USSR itself could be called an association from which no one is permitted to withdraw, since it is a criminal offense for a citizen to leave Soviet territory without permission.

It is depressing to compare the USSR Academy of Sciences to a thieves' artel, but it seems appropriate to recall here the reaction in 1948 when Sir Henry Dale sent a letter

---

* A thief is allowed to go straight only if he has the consent of his fellows; otherwise turning one's back on crime is often punished by death. Soviet courts regard the murder of such reformed criminals by their former confederates as "committed in connection with the victim's performance of his social duty" which is an aggravating circumstance for homicide (Article 102 of the Criminal Code). In labor camps, the death penalty may be imposed on recidivists who hinder fellow convicts from "embarking on the path of reform" (Article 77–1 of the Criminal Code). A recent example is the case of one Galatkin, who was convicted under this Article for inflicting knife wounds on an orderly in a "strict-regime colony" in order, as he admitted, to "prevent his victim from adopting a conscientious attitude towards labor." (Reported in the *Bulletin of the RSFSR Supreme Court* (1974), No. 9.)

resigning as an honorary member of the Academy in protest against the persecution of geneticists in the USSR. A motion was passed at a plenary meeting of the Academy depriving Dale of honorary membership, since he had "become an obedient tool of anti-democratic forces." The resignation of Professor H. J. Muller, an American geneticist, elicited a similar reaction.*

In his *History of the Pugachev Rebellion*, Pushkin gave an example of the artel system among the first Cossacks, who in many respects were the forerunners of the underworld:

> The Yaik Cossacks were obedient to the authorities in Moscow, but among themselves they held to their original method of self-government. All enjoyed equal rights; the *atamans* and elders were elected by the community as temporary executors of its will; councils were held at which every Cossack was free to speak, and all matters of common concern were decided by majority vote; there were no written ordinances; treason, cowardice, murder, and theft were punished in the same way—"into the sack, then into the water." Such were the chief features of the Cossack regime.

The system of association among the seventeenth-century Cossacks is typical of the beginnings of any society of free and equal members. The ataman or chief was no more than *primus inter pares*, and however great his authority, he could be replaced at any time. Emphasizing his dependence on the community, Pushkin wrote of the Cossack leader:

> Pugachev was not an autocrat. The Yaik Cossacks who originated the revolt controlled the activities of the leader who had come amongst them with no other distinction than his exceptional boldness and some

* George Counts and Nucia Lodge, *The Country of the Blind* (Boston, 1949).

> knowledge of the art of war. He did nothing without
> the Cossacks' approval, whereas they often acted with-
> out his knowledge and sometimes against his wishes.
> They paid him external respect: in public they walked
> behind him bareheaded and bowed obsequiously; but
> in private they treated him as a companion, sitting
> beside him in shirtsleeves and with their caps on, get-
> ting drunk together and singing rivermen's ballads.
> Pugachev chafed under their guardianship and used
> to complain that he "lived in a narrow street."*

Although artels began with the principle of equal rights
among the members, as time went on this tended to disappear. Human nature is such that persons who have attained
a position of leadership, even a temporary one, do their best
to consolidate and protect it. This often means altering the
legal or ethical basis of the association, which, as a rule, is
more easily done by a group of leaders than by one alone.
Hence a collective authority is instituted—an elite that is no
longer chosen by the whole community but is self-perpetu-
ating, its ranks filled by its own choice.

In the criminal world, where members were dispersed
throughout the community, the emergence of an elite was a
more complicated and gradual process, probably connected
with mutual recognition by the bosses of what were the
strongest and most active associations. The evidence suggests, however, that a Russian criminal elite is far from a
recent phenomenon, and surely organized gangs of thieves
were among the first.

According to the Soviet scholar D. S. Likhachev:

> The *milieu* of professional thieves is, first and foremost,
> that of individuals with no social position, the *Lum-*

---

* The case of Pugachev is especially interesting as he claimed to be
the rightful czar and was so proclaimed in the Cossack community, which
would have made it awkward to replace him by electing another leader;
this perhaps is why his associates exercised close control over his actions.

penproletariat. However, while the *Lumpenproletariat*
is a phenomenon met with in almost every phase of
social development up to the present time, the existence of a self-contained underworld belongs especially
to the era when the mass expropriation of land from
the peasants, and hence their rapid pauperization,
created the first preconditions of capitalist accumulation. This "prelude to the revolution, which was to lay
the foundation of the capitalist mode of production,
dates from the last third of the fifteenth and the first
decades of the sixteenth century" (*Capital,* Vol. I,
chapter 26), and it is at that time that we encounter
the first evidence of thieves' *argot.*[10]

At the present time the elite of the Russian criminal
world are the so-called regulars (*vory v zakone,* literally,
"thieves professing the code") who maintain constant
liaison with one another. From time to time some of them
hold congresses. I last heard of a congress in the early six-
ties; there may have been others since. I do not know how
often they occur, but it does not appear to be annually or at
any fixed interval.

Outsiders know little of what goes on at these meetings,
but those who have studied the underworld believe that they
deal with disputes between gangs (of which there are
many) over each other's territory of operations and so on,
and with upholding the thieves' code and, if necessary,
adapting it to changing circumstances. Quite possibly the
admission of new members is also discussed. There is not
much information available about the procedure whereby a
common thief becomes a regular, but it is my impression
that it varies from case to case.

It is also not known to what extent the elite is divided
into categories of rank. However, the information I have
suggests that relations between the bosses are not formally
defined but depend on age, personal standing, and such

qualities as prowess. But even outstanding leaders do not appear to have any special rights when it comes to making decisions.

I am purposely underlining the points about which I am not certain, at least partially to illustrate the difficulty of describing a closed society with its own laws and customs. The task is made even more difficult by the constant jockeying for position among the elite, who exploit the ambiguities of the traditional code for their own advantage. The actual character of an association generally remains closer to its tradition if the structure of authority is pyramidal, that is, if a single person controls the association and all its parts. But the Soviet underworld is organized more democratically, or at least more collectively.

The separate parts of the Russian criminal community are governed by elected leaders on the artel principle, but the elections are not necessarily formal. A thieves' artel often forms around an authoritative personality who is naturally chosen as leader. If such a person joins an already existing artel in which there is no other strong personality, he may be elected leader by tacit consent, even though he has not laid claim to the office. In societies governed by custom, such recognition often replaces formal elections, and the same thing is apt to take place in workers' artels. Of course, there are cases where thieves contend for the mastery of a particular group, and in that event the decision usually depends on physical force rather than past experience or better knowledge of the thieves' code. The rest of the group follow the fight as they might follow an election meeting, and usually the victorious combatant is declared leader.

However, as I have said, he is a leader among equals. Although we do not know how complicated the criminal hierarchy is, there are at least three classes: the elite, the rank and file, and the apprentices who, if they prove themselves, will one day become full-fledged thieves. A still lower category of middlemen—receivers, casers, shelterers of thieves—is not, strictly speaking, part of the underworld but forms a link between it and normal society.

Full-fledged thieves do not recognize apprentices, amateurs, or middlemen as equals. A gang in which only the leader is a regular criminal will be run on strictly authoritarian lines. Most of the gangs that political prisoners had a chance to observe in camps and penitentiaries were of this kind, and this led to a false impression that all thieves' gangs were equally dictatorial.

Thieves' artels composed of regulars have an elected leadership and, like other artels, observe a kind of collective responsibility. They also allow members to leave and join other gangs. This could hardly be otherwise, since thieves frequently move from place to place, either for better pickings or to escape the police. As in ordinary artels, thieves' profits are generally distributed equally, though an exception may be made if one member has done the lion's share of the work. Auxiliaries who do not belong to the artel are paid by agreement. Apparently there is no great trouble in dividing the spoils; mutual aid is a strong principle, and thieves in the Soviet Union are generally indifferent to the accumulation of wealth. The monetary needs of a thieves' den are met by contributions from its members according to their ability; there does not appear to be any fixed scale, although occasional quarrels over the division of the spoils do occur.

The groups or gangs which I have called artels are given various names by the thieves themselves. In St. Petersburg in the last century they were called choirs, and each met at its own tavern where the gang's funds were also collected.

It is never easy to discover all the unwritten laws that govern associations that rely heavily on custom even if such associations are not secret. But if one studies various cases in which such laws have been applied, certain basic principles, which the members respect with almost religious fervor, emerge. The code that governs the Soviet underworld stems mainly from the fact that its members live in a state of isolation from normal society and reject its obligations. The specific purpose of "thieves' law" is to define the exact limits of the isolation and the rejection.

This may surprise the reader who assumes that the thieves' chief commandment is simply "Thou shalt steal." This is, however, not the case. A gang member is free to live without stealing. If he is on the run, he may live in the forest on berries and wild animals without breaking the thieves' law, but he will be deemed a traitor if he enters into any of the social ties that have been forbidden to him. The denial of the right of ownership is in itself a way of rejecting social obligations. A religious hermit may choose to live apart from society without repudiating society's legal and moral principles and his fellow humans' rights of property. A member of a thieves' gang cannot.

It is hard to enumerate all the social ties that are forbidden by thieves' law, or to say in which cases a thief is merely disapproved of and in which he is regarded as an out-and-out transgressor of the thieves' law. It is, for example, a definite violation of thieves' law to cooperate with the State authorities in any way. This applies whether or not this cooperation directly harms the underworld, although, of course, special penalties attach to such activities as informing on one's associates or providing assistance to prison or camp officials. A thief who commits any of these crimes is an outcast, a scab or turncoat (the Russian word literally means bitch); he is judged by a court of his former colleagues, and the only possible sentence is death, generally by the infliction of multiple stab wounds. A thief may commit a crime and be unpunished by the law of the land, he may even escape from jail or from a labor camp, but he knows that it is almost impossible to escape judgment by a thieves' court.*

During World War II, thieves were conscripted by the thousands, but those who served their country in this way were all branded as scabs and, according to thieves' law, were liable to extermination on their return. They were so numerous, however, that they challenged the verdict; the so-called scabs' war took place, and its result was to soften the ban against thieves enlisting in their country's service.

The charge leveled against those who fought in World War II was that they had put on uniforms and carried rifles —the symbol of a prison warden's authority. The fact that they had protected their country from a foreign invader counted for nothing, or rather aggravated the offense, since a thief's detachment from society extends to ethical norms such as patriotism. Thieves are not, in this sense, *against* patriotism, nor are they against their own or any other country; it is simply that there is no such thing as patriotism in their moral vocabulary. If there were, it would constitute a link between them and the rest of society. This is worth emphasizing, as Soviet novels have more than once depicted thieves as patriots—men who had cut loose from society but nevertheless made the right choice between serving their country and serving the enemy. All that I know of the criminal world leads me to think that such stories are simply wish fulfillment.

The story of the "patriotic thief" usually follows a familiar form: a foreign spy tries to recruit a Soviet criminal for intelligence purposes, and the latter, after much mental anguish, remembers his patriotic duty and refuses. Actu-

* Victor Kabachnik, a recent Russian émigré who served a term of exile in Siberia, has told me that a thief may shield his comrades during interrogation not out of bravery but out of cowardice, as he well knows what retribution would follow if he informed on them.

ally, serving a foreign state is no less contrary to thieves'
law than serving one's own.

Lev Sheinin's *Notes of a Criminal Investigator* contains
many improbable examples of such incidents. In one case he
describes a gang of thieves helping the police recover a watch
stolen from a pro-Soviet French politician. The thieves debate in boy scout fashion about the honor of their home-
town, and the aged fence clinches the matter—with somewhat greater realism—by saying: "It's a political matter,
and your lives won't be worth living until the watch is returned."

As far as everyday life is concerned, the principle of detachment means that a thief will not join an ordinary citizen
for any purpose whatsoever. Criminals are remarkably
honest among themselves, but they are quite untrustworthy
in their dealings with "straight guys," to whom they end-
lessly lie and make false promises. The only exception is the
paracriminal class already mentioned, the fences and other
middlemen who enable thieves to be in society but not of it.
Without this class it would be impossible for thieves to enter
into any economic relation with normal society; they would
be confined to a, so to speak, natural economy, stealing
food, clothing and other necessities as and when they
needed them, or else stealing only money. As it is, they can
sell their spoils and convert into money such objects as they
have no use for. Fences have to be people the criminals can
trust implicitly, and they know that if they betray that trust
they will get short shrift. At the same time they are despised
by thieves, whose moral code is so contrary to all ideas of
avarice and accumulation that they refuse to haggle with
receivers and accept ludicrously low sums in return for
their booty.*

* Naturally the market for stolen goods is subject to its own special
laws. Receivers generally take the precaution of selling them to other
receivers, who choose their customers carefully. It is a risky business and
rates a high commission, so the thief himself does not get much.

Other members of the paracriminal class are those who provide thieves with hideouts and meeting places, and those who tip them off about likely opportunities for theft.

Apart from these auxiliaries, whose activity is, of course, illegal, criminals may show a measure of confidence in law-abiding citizens who have helped them out of tight spots or won their admiration by toughness and independence of character. This has been known to apply to political prisoners in the camps, although generally speaking the attitude of common criminals toward politicals is one of contempt and mockery. It is rare for a "straight guy" to earn a criminal's respect, either in the camps or in ordinary life, since even if he possesses the right qualities he may not have a chance of displaying them in a way the criminal can understand. Members of the underworld are accustomed to coarseness of manner, and it is hard for them to find a common language with educated people even if they are fellow prisoners, except on those occasions when thieves are in a sentimental mood and find solace in dramatic, highly colored confessions.

It can also happen that thieves develop a special relationship toward ordinary citizens who have no influence or property, like soldiers in the ranks, for instance. According to Max Hayward, a Senior Fellow at St. Antony's College, Oxford, a thieves' congress held shortly before the Nazi attack on the Soviet Union ruled that military personnel were not to be molested. This decision was probably inspired not by patriotism, but by either a kind of sympathy or the fear of exceptionally severe reprisals.

A thief and his associates are forbidden any attachments that might limit the thief's freedom to act. A thief's wife is allowed practically no social relations with the normal world; she is her husband's property, or rather his and his fellow thieves', and if he goes to prison she will generally cohabit with one of them, while continuing to take an interest in the prisoner's welfare—monogamy is not excluded by the thieves' code, but it is seldom lasting. Thieves' wives are not prostitutes, though at their husband's command they may satisfy the needs of others. Prostitutes may also associate with gangs, but as a rule they are not required to sever their connections with ordinary society; they may return to a lawful occupation or combine it with prostitution if they so desire.

If a criminal's wife violates her obligations, she is warned and, in the cases of obstinacy, punished by death. While subject to many rules of conduct, these women have no place in the hierarchy of thieves: they are not despised, like prostitutes or honest citizens, but they have no special rights and are lucky if their fidelity and devotion are repaid by gratitude. The relationship of a thief and his wife is that of master and slave, except that the slave has voluntarily chosen her lot, recognizing the preeminence of a strong man and his right to use her as he pleases.

While the wife's initial choice may be voluntary, she is, of course, no more able to secede from the criminal community than her husband. However, she enjoys considerable prestige among women connected with the underworld, and many prostitutes' highest ambition is to become a thief's wife.*

The one way in which a thief's wife may earn respect is by becoming the mother of a future thief. Varlam Shalamov, a prisoner in Stalin's camps and now a Soviet author, in "Women of the Underworld,"[11] expresses disbelief in the thieves' reverence for motherhood on the basis of his own impressions and the somewhat dubious aphorism, "A cult of motherhood that does not extend to wives and

---

* *The Moscow Underworld* (1924) described the position of such women gangsters: "In lean times these women maintain their husbands by prostitution and by robbing clients. Although they often show great devotion to their men, they have to put up with a great deal from them and are treated as scapegoats when a 'job' is unsuccessful or goes wrong through someone else's fault."

women in general is spurious." My information does not
bear out his opinion. Cases are known in which a thief who
was hard pressed by the police risked arrest in order to visit
and help his mother. There is a good deal of evidence that
thieves do not cultivate paternal feelings or care much
about children; but they take it for granted that a thief's son
will become a thief and his daughter a companion of thieves,
although this does not always happen, especially nowadays. A "born thief" in this sense enjoys a privileged position in the hierarchy, and some believe that as a rule only
those who belong to this category can become regulars.

The thief's desire to be untrammeled by family ties is
appropriate to his way of life with its frequent alarms,
changes of abode, and spells in prison, which may exceed in
the aggregate his years of liberty. Apart from these practical reasons, it accords with the general thieves' rule of detachment from social obligations. In this way the modern
Soviet criminal world resembles the early Cossacks, whose
attitude toward the family was described by Pushkin:

> According to legend, the Cossacks were once so de-
> voted to bachelorhood that they agreed to kill all their
> children and abandon their wives every time they set
> off on a new campaign. The first to transgress this
> cruel law by sparing his young wife was a chief named
> Gugnya. Following his example, the Cossacks suc-
> cumbed to the yoke of domesticity, and today the en-
> lightened and hospitable inhabitants of the banks of
> the Urals drink toasts to the memory of "grandmother
> Gugnya."

The unwritten thieves' law governs relations within the
criminal community. Likhachev, who studied the behavior
of convicts building the Baltic–White Sea canal during the
early 1930s, observed:

> Behavior among thieves is regulated and circumscribed
> by innumerable rules, standards and notions of pro-

priety and good manners, all interrelated in an intricate hierarchy. Any violation of these rules is punished by a thieves' court, which has its own procedure. The penalty is always severe and inflicted without delay. The thieves' community has tremendous authority over the individual. Despite thieves' apparent lack of discipline, their lives are governed by a network of strict regulations that extend to the most minute matters, and ultimately by a system of "collective beliefs" that is remarkably uniform among criminals with different ethnic roots.[12]

All regular thieves are honest and helpful in their dealings with one another, but the paracriminal population practice deceit and theft on one another and are chary with assistance. Observers of these classes have sometimes been misled into imagining that their behavior was typical of thieves. However, the latter's solidarity is well attested, and political prisoners in Stalin's camps were often surprised at the cooperation that developed between thieves who had not known each other before. Mutual aid was at a premium in camp conditions, and many believed that thieves displayed more of it than politicals.

Thieves' attitude toward property rights is very interesting. They seem either to deny such rights altogether or to have no sense of them. As a rule they attach little or no importance to owning property themselves, however strange this may seem in people who go to great trouble and risk long terms of imprisonment to steal from others. They are not interested in thrift, that is, in saving and keeping property, which is what the sense of ownership means to most people. On the contrary, they seem to want to get rid of things as soon as they have acquired them. Their pleasure comes not from possessing stolen objects but from the long and strenuous efforts that are necessary to acquire them. However successful the theft and however large the booty, the thief may gamble it away in a night, spend it on women or drink, or use it all to help a fellow thief. The facts that thieves do not steal from one another and that a down-and-out thief can be sure that his comrades will come to his rescue and not expect repayment reflect this indifference to property. At the same time, thieves' property is not held in common. A thief's goods are his own and not automatically available to his fellows or to the gang, but he regards them as temporary possessions and does not mind parting with them.*

On the other hand, he may violate the property rights of those below him in the hierarchy, at any rate those of his womenfolk, who, along with all their possessions, belong to him.

Accounts of thieves often suggest that they are as careless of human life as they are of the rights of property. This is an exaggeration, although their ideas on the subject certainly differ from those of conventional morality. They do not like messy jobs and prefer to steal without killing. If they have to, they will kill anyone, especially someone who interferes with a robbery by alerting the public or the police, but their desire to avoid murder is not simply because of the heavy penalties for armed robbery. Most thieves are not bloodthirsty by nature, nor does their code require them to be, and their behavior depends on many circumstances. In general they set no store by the life of an ordinary citizen, but they will kill him only if there is good reason to, in which case they do it without hesitation. They feel no

* S. Maximov, in his account of nineteenth-century convicts, describes tramps' attitude toward the right of ownership in a way that parallels that of the thieves' communities today. And, like thieves, tramps maintain a strict hierarchy in a prison society as he describes it. "The life of destitution and the long marches from one prison to another have deadened the tramp's sense of property, which becomes something alien and even repulsive to him. He does not covet or steal the property of others and has no sense of his own."

compunction in killing thieves who turn traitor and are sentenced to death by a thieves' court, although these executions are usually performed collectively.

Thieves respect courage and hold their own lives in contempt. The saying, "It's your turn today, mine tomorrow," which thieves apply to their victims, is usually regarded as a mockery, but it reflects a certain light-heartedness on the thief's part toward his own death as well.

Like many closed societies, the Russian underworld has its own language. Its grammatical structure is Russian—whether correctly spoken or not is another matter—but its vocabulary is different, and those who use it fluently may to all intents and purposes dispense with Russian words altogether.

Some authorities call it an artificial language, but this seems hardly appropriate for a speech that has lasted for centuries and has developed according to the same kind of laws as natural languages do. Since I am concerned here not with philology but only with giving an account of the special thieves' vocabulary that will throw some light on their conditions and way of life, I have not confined myself to the present time but have gone back to nineteenth-century terms as well.

It has been suggested that modern thieves' argot is based on the language (*ofeni*)* of nineteenth-century peddlers who went from village to village selling icons, broadsheets, and other items. Craftsmen in many parts of Russia used this language when they wanted to be unintelligible to outsiders. Contemporary thieves' slang certainly contains words found in ofen glossaries, but it has also borrowed from other private languages used in various parts of Russia, particularly sailors' slang, which is to some extent in-

---

* Singular *ofenya*, word of dubious origin. It may be a corruption of "Athenian."—*Translator's note.*

ternational, as well as Yiddish, Romany, and the languages of neighboring peoples to the east and west.

Beggars in old Russia also had a language of their own which varied from one part of the country to another and showed many traces of ofen influence. Around the turn of the century it began to be replaced by a kind of Pig Latin based on the insertion of meaningless syllables in standard words. The new jargon was not so impenetrable as the old, but it was quite difficult for the uninitiated to follow, especially when spoken quickly.

Both ofen and the old beggars' language had a large vocabulary, which was not confined to purely technical subjects. The argot of modern thieves seems to be more restricted in this respect, although it also contains words for everyday things.*

I have collected somewhere over a thousand words of thieves' argot. Some of them are ordinary Russian vulgarisms; others belong to the language of camps and prisons, which was formerly thought of as a special dialect. Today conditions have changed and there is a good deal of overlapping between prison speech and thieves' slang.†

It is quite possible that the words known to me are only a pale reflection of the language spoken by top criminals, which is a secret from outsiders. Criminals of middle rank whose conversations I heard from time to time mingled argot and ordinary Russian, just as specialists intersperse technical terms in their conversation. In any case it is im-

---

* Philologists have disputed as to whether it should be called a professional language—not only because of doubts about whether thieving is a profession, but also because thieves' argot is clearly different in kind from the elliptical but standard Russian used by railroadmen and other technicians.

† Cf. *Soviet Prison Camp Speech*, compiled by Meyer Galler and Harlan E. Marquess (Madison: University of Wisconsin Press, 1972).[13] This book contains many common vulgarisms as well as thieves' slang and language peculiar to the camps.

possible to compile an up-to-date glossary of thieves' argot
because the whole point of the language is that it is unintelligible to informers and others; so as soon as words become
known to the authorities they are dropped from the vocabulary.* When this happens they are replaced not by new
coinages but by synonyms, of which there are many. Apparently at any given time only part of the vocabulary is
used, and this makes it easier to detect police agents who
may try to infiltrate the criminal world but whose knowledge of argot is out of date.

Thieves' slang also helps to distinguish different ranks of
the hierarchy. When so many amateurs with a superficial
knowledge of thieves' customs pretend to belong to the
underworld, a way has to be found to keep them at a distance. Impostors are guarded against by frequent exchanges
of information among genuine thieves, who can check a
newcomer's story about other thieves he has known in
prison or worked with; but a still surer method is to probe
his knowledge of thieves' slang.

A glossary of thieves' slang, issued by the government to
the Kiev police in 1964, is appended to the Russian edition

* Some authorities do not agree that secrecy is the language's main
raison d'être. For instance, the Soviet philologist D. S. Likhachev states:
"It is naive to suppose that a criminal can preserve secrecy by talking
thieves' argot, since by doing so he betrays the fact that he is a thief.
Generally thieves use this language only among themselves and not in
public." I think this is an exaggeration. As far back as Pushkin's time
(see his "The Captain's Daughter") thieves used their own jargon in public in cases of necessity. By doing so they might betray the fact that they
were thieves, but they did not furnish any positive evidence against themselves.

Anyway, in former times thieves did not conceal the fact that they
were criminals; this has become the norm only in the last few decades,
when thieves have also stopped wearing a distinctive costume. As Likhachev himself wrote in the 1930s, "a thief takes pride in drawing attention
to himself by wearing the fashionable attire of his profession with a cap
pulled over his eyes, by his gait and gestures and, finally, by tattooing
himself, despite the fact that this makes him a target of police suspicion."

of this book.* Here I will confine myself to listing some of the concepts for which slang terms exist.

Thieves' language comprises, first of all, terms for the criminal world and its members, for gang leaders and bosses and for the exercise of the profession. The leader of a gang of thieves is known to them by his real name; it is not thought ethical to conceal it, and there would be no point in doing so. A thief in charge of a gang of irregulars uses the cover name Ivan. The head of a gang of women thieves is called Masha. (Such gangs are rare and are treated with respect, unlike thieves' wives and prostitutes. A typical member of one of these groups is described by Varlam Shalamov in his tale "Women of the Underworld.")

There are special terms for a mate, or thief of equal status, for those of junior rank, for apprentices, and for those who train them. There are words for those who shield their comrades during investigation and for those who give them away. Informers, as already mentioned, are known as bitches, and their prison cells are "doghouses" (they are kept in solitary confinement to prevent retribution from other prisoners). A thief's oath begins "I'll be a bitch if . . . ," and twenty-five years ago—I do not know about today —it was accompanied by a special gesture: the right thumb flicked against the front teeth and then moved in a circle around the subject's chin. Other special gestures were used to warn a speaker that a certain subject was dangerous. According to Maximov,[14] thieves used to swear by "convict's honor," but I doubt that there is any corresponding expression today.

There is a term for a thieves' court and for those who carry out its sentences. Minor offenders are beaten by their fellows and, in token of submission, often have to stand with arms raised. There is a term for this gesture and a variety of terms for beating, slashing with a razor, and so

* *Ugolovnaya Rossiya* (New York: Khronika Press, 1977).

on, and also for the execution of traitors and other serious offenders.

Other terms are associated with the division of spoils (equitable or otherwise), hideouts, meeting places, and the custody of stolen goods. A wide range of vocabulary denotes different kinds of thieves and their assistants: pickpockets; railroad-station and cloakroom thieves; cat burglars, slender youths who can climb through windows; shoplifters; raiders of food stores; hat snatchers; baggage thieves; train robbers; robbers of funeral guests, prostitutes' clients, and drunks; safebreakers; and "guest artists" who travel about plying their trade in different cities. The special deftness required of a pickpocket is reflected in various terms for the man and his activity, his fingers, the art of feeling a prospect's clothes, the special knife used for slitting pockets, the newspaper or parcel behind which stolen objects are concealed, the moment of success, the reaction of the victim who realizes he or she has been robbed, etc. There is also a term for each pocket of a man's suit.

Other expressions denote the criminal's tools—jimmy, fret saw, skeleton keys, diamond for cutting glass—and papers, money, and valuables, especially watches of all kinds. There are special terms for the thief's victims and for the official world, its authorities and processes—and this section of the vocabulary, as might be expected, is not especially complimentary.

"A group, swapping experiences, would fall to boasting, and the next thing you knew, they'd be at each other's throats."*

This quotation from a female prisoner's diary is typical of the atmosphere of thieves' meetings, whether in jail or outside. The main theme of their boasting is their boldness

* *The Moscow Underworld* (Moscow, 1924), p. 23.

and ingenuity, which would come under the heading of professional pride in other walks of life.* As elsewhere, this professionalism is linked with the existence of a hierarchy, and the type of conduct that is most admired is that associated with its upper ranks.

Apart from professional skill and observance of the thieves' code, thieves attach special importance to the ability to endure the pain and suffering inevitable in a community that is at war with the rest of society.† In some cases this endurance is carried beyond the bounds of practical necessity and becomes an end in itself, with manifestations that are senseless and frightening to an outside observer. Prisoners often practice self-torture to a degree that is unknown among thieves at liberty.‡ Edward Kuznetsov, now serving a fifteen-year sentence for his participation in the attempt to hijack a plane and fly it to Sweden in 1970, has described terrible instances of self-mutilation practiced by convicts.§

> I have many times witnessed some of the most fantastic instances of self-mutilation. I have seen convicts swallow huge numbers of nails and quantities of barbed wire; I have seen them swallow mercury thermometers, pewter tureens (after first breaking them

* An instance is known of a thief who was so proud of his performance that he telephoned the police chief and boasted that he was uncatchable, whereupon he was caught.[15]

† Many have suggested that thieves are better able to endure physical pain because their level of sensitivity is low. This may be so, but it is hard to generalize. Among noncriminals too, endurance of pain may often be due to insensitivity, just as courage is often due to lack of foresight or imagination.

‡ In the latter case, self-inflicted pain is part of a thief's normal training in self-defense. For instance, he has to learn how to catch a knife that is thrown at him and to fling it back at the assailant. As I know from observation, a man practicing this art must anticipate painful flesh wounds.

§ Edward Kuznetsov, *Prison Diaries* (New York, 1975), p. 169.

up into "edible" portions), chess pieces, dominoes, needles, ground glass, spoons, knives, and many other objects. I have seen convicts sew up their lips or eyelids with thread and wire; sew rows of buttons to their bodies; nail their scrotums to a bed; or swallow a nail bent like a hook, and then attach this hook to the door by a piece of thread so that the door cannot be opened without pulling the "fish" inside out. I have seen convicts cut open the skin on their arms or legs and peel it off as if it were a stocking, or cut lumps of flesh from their belly or their thighs, roast them and eat them; or let the blood drip from a slit vein into a tureen, crumble bread crumbs into it and then gulp it down like a bowl of soup; or cover themselves with paper and set fire to themselves; or cut off their fingers or nose or ears or penis—there is absolutely nothing they will not do.

Kuznetsov discounts the idea that self-torture is a protest on the part of desperate men, believing it is rather a way to "carve a slice out of life"—for example, the convict gets a chance to go to the hospital and see the nurses swing their hips; he gets off work for a while, receives parcels, a special diet and drugs. No doubt there is something in this, but it seems to me that the frenzy of self-torture exceeds all practical calculation. I see it mainly as an attempt to prove personal courage, which is so important to a thief's self-esteem and to the respect in which he is held by others. The desire for prestige is so strong that a thief who cannot acquire esteem in some other way resorts to the method of savage self-mutilation.

It is improbable that we will ever get much information about the widespread self-mutilation in Soviet camps and prisons. Soviet publications say little about the practice, though it is mentioned from time to time, e.g., in *Problems of Crime*, Series 15 (Moscow, 1972), and Felix Yaroshevsky, a doctor who recently emigrated from the USSR, has published an article on the subject in the *Journal of the*

Canadian Psychiatric Association, Vol. 20, No. 6 (1975).

Nineteenth-century convicts practiced self-torture to a lesser degree—although still sufficient to horrify normal people—for practical ends such as getting off work or into the hospital. In our day, a self-respecting thief will not maim himself for a merely practical purpose, although he is not above shamming illness (and often threatening the doctor in the bargain). It is not clear, in fact, how often the stories of self-mutilation involve regular thieves; the prison camp population is a motley one, but insofar as regulars do engage in these practices, it is likely to be for prestige rather than practical reasons.

Thieves had many opportunities to show courage in the scabs' war, which I have already mentioned, and which is described in some detail in a *samizdat* manuscript* by Varlam Shalamov. The opportunities were perhaps greatest for regulars, who had a choice of being killed or adopting the new scabs' law, whereas the scabs, when defeated, were simply killed as traitors. Andrei Sinyavsky, the Soviet literary critic who spent almost six years in Soviet prison camps for sending his works abroad for publication under the pseudonym Abram Tertz, in *A Voice from the Chorus* (New York, 1976) describes the courageous end of a thief named Pushkin:

> When the scab laid him on a sheet of iron and lit a fire underneath, he shouted out words that I would be proud to use as a motto, if only I felt worthy of them: "Hey, tell everybody that I died a thief!"

However, as the scabs won in the end, apparently some "orthodox" thieves preferred apostasy to a glorious death. The ex-thief Alexei Frolov obviously was describing those melancholy days when he wrote:

* *Samizdat*, a manuscript circulated by unofficial means in the Soviet Union—*Translator's note*.

I saw the whole thing. A father and his son might be on different sides, and one of them would have to knuckle under or be killed. It was a fierce fight, without pity or conscience. I remember men being threatened with knives, the ax or the rope, and made to kneel and strip themselves of all human dignity.[16]

Even when not at war, criminals are not distinguished by refined taste or delicate manners—on the contrary, their code of behavior sets a premium on toughness. This is especially true in sexual matters, where brute force is not tempered by any vestige of tenderness as it is in even the coarsest spheres of regular society. In the thieves' world, the most highly valued expression of the sexual instinct seems to be rape, especially collective rape. (For this, as for the sexual act in general, thieves' slang has a variety of terms over and above the "obscenities" of standard Russian.)

Even with their wives or prostitutes, thieves like to give an impression of violence. This is also common among noncriminals, of course, but thieves are even more inclined to beat their female companions, and sadism among them appears to be not only widespread but deliberately cultivated. At the same time, there is a certain playfulness of language in their terms for sexual organs. And, as I have mentioned, the men's roughness does not prevent their wives from being devoted to them, or prostitutes from aspiring to marry them.

Thieves' language has special words for dancing, drinking, and other amusements, particularly card-playing and, in the south, crap-shooting (for which the Georgians also have a term of their own). Among the terms used for a deck of cards is "bible": this goes back to the days when prisoners made cards out of the pages of Bibles, the form in which paper was most often available to them.

Cards have long been popular with criminals. In the seventeenth century, prison wardens were instructed to prevent prisoners "dicing and card-playing."[17] According to Maximov, tramps in prison—who, as much evidence shows, correspond to the regular thieves of the present day—enjoyed the privilege of being granted credit for gambling by their companions.

> A tramp can use a brick or his own fist as a pledge, in consideration of which visible sign he is accorded a credit of one and a half silver rubles. . . . He is trusted on his "convict's word of honor." Once a month the "bank" passes, and according to the rules every debt is wiped out at that stage; but if the tramp becomes banker, debts to him remain in force.[18]

Prison diversions also include homosexuality, which was prevalent among convicts in former times and is still common in camps today. According to one researcher into the subject in the 1920s, young men were generally seduced with favors of all kinds, gifts of food, etc., but were treated with contempt as soon as the seduction had taken place; their active partners, on the other hand, were much admired.[19]

In the 1930s and 1940s the only difference was that there was no need to seduce, but merely to threaten with a knife. At this period, boys of twelve were sentenced to labor camps, and many were turned into homosexuals. Corruption of youths by older prisoners is still widespread in the Soviet Union—and indeed in other countries as well.

Criminals who become active pederasts in prison generally remain so after their release, rather than reaccustom themselves to women. Lesbianism is equally common among female prisoners.

There has been no study of wall drawings and graffiti in Russian prisons, so far as I know. Apart from these, the only visual art practiced in the underworld is tattooing. This, too, has been very little studied, but it appears to have not only an esthetic but a psychosocial significance connected with the individual's status in the underworld hierarchy. Tattoos became closely identified with the criminal world, and most tattooing was done in prison.

According to Soviet publications of the 1920s, when the subject was not yet banned, prisoners generally had themselves tattooed out of boredom.[20,21]

Subjects observed by M. Avdeyeva in her study of prison tattoos include naked women in various poses (only three of them "coarse," as she puts it), a mermaid, women's heads, women in clothes, eagles, a heart pierced by an arrow, chains, cupids, various mottoes, a sailor with a lady, a dog chasing a woman, a couple dancing the tango, skulls, Death with a scythe, a tomb with the inscription "Sleep, Mother, and wait for me," a church with the words round it, "Manya, forgive me—Kolya Klimov." Another tattoo consisted of a naked woman standing on three books with arms raised aloft while another woman in a mantle kneels with head bowed over the books and holds the first woman's hand; the inscription is, "You have gone away and left me alone"—this was tattooed after the man's wife had been shot for looting. Other subjects that have been noted are a sword with the motto "All's one—I'm ready for anything"; two swords with the legends "I will avenge you" and "Farewell, my dreams, she is no more"; Cupid and Psyche; an eagle with a sailor in its claws; a pig playing the fiddle; a cat and mouse on the buttocks, the mouse apparently fleeing into the man's anus; a woman kneeling before a cross with a ship, the sun, and a lighthouse in the distance.

Present-day subjects are probably simpler and cruder than these, but Andrei Sinyavsky noted one remarkable exception in the labor camp where he served his sentence: an eagle tearing at Prometheus's breast and, in the background, a dog copulating with a lady.

Tattoos with political themes, e.g., "Slave of the Communist Party," are described by the former prisoner Anatoly Marchenko in his book, *My Testimony* (New York, 1969), pp.198–99.

Gernet makes the following observation on the esthetic quality of Russian tattooing in his article on Moscow prison tattoos (1924):

> Comparing what we have read concerning the tattooing of foreign criminals with what we have observed in the case of Russian ones, the latter seem to be more original. The world record appears to be held by the inmate of a Moscow prison on whose chest was tattooed a reproduction of Vasnetsov's picture *The Three Warriors*. . . . As far as we know, no foreign criminal has had the idea of turning himself into a living Old Master.

4

The Soviet
Authorities and the
Underworld

Nothing so annoys professionals of any kind as to be aped by amateurs and dilettantes. At all periods in history they have erected barriers against such people and against the too rapid advancement of apprentices, as the organization of the medieval craft guilds amply demonstrates. The motive is not so much fear of competition as concern for the honor, integrity and reputation of the profession. The Russian underworld is no exception to this rule, and it has resisted all claims of unauthorized persons to belong to it, including those who are attracted to the underworld by a romantic desire to benefit society, a desire fostered by popular legends about famous brigands who were also liberators.

The course of Russian history has been such that in the final contest between regular and amateur criminals, the latter won. This has by degrees demoralized and disorganized criminal society. The amateurs' victory did not allow others to penetrate the underworld; the regulars were strong enough to prevent that. What happened was that during the Revolution amateurs took over the State itself, including its punitive apparatus for subduing criminals. Fighting crime was not, however, the new rulers' first objective. On the contrary, they came to terms with the underworld after a fashion, releasing its members from prison and declaring them to be socially kindred elements. In return, they hoped that the criminals would find the new regime socially acceptable and would cease to exercise their profession at its expense.

The underworld does not seem to have been disconcerted at first by the amateurs' seizure of power. Criminals are not interested in politics. They seem to have regarded the social affinity they were offered as something of a joke, although they hoped it would enlarge their freedom of action. But in fact this doctrine was the new regime's first successful move toward controlling the underworld. Up until then the Russian State and the underworld had been at daggers with each other. Their only contact was the punitive measures the State took against criminals. When the new regime invited contacts of a different sort, some criminals responded, either inspired by the idea of national liberation or hoping for plunder on a larger scale than before. Some became government employees and even joined the State security apparatus. The underworld leaders naturally objected to this and took revenge on the deserters whenever they could. As far as I can discover, the number of scabs was not great, but it was sufficient to demoralize criminal society, even though the new regime's objectives and methods were similar in many ways to those of the underworld. The difference was that the State plundered private homes and churches more boldly than brigands of the past had ever dreamed of doing, but it did so on the basis of published decrees.

In those troubled times nearly all Russia's traditional institutions were destroyed or radically transformed. Only a few organizations, independent of the State and fairly conservative in structure, survived the deluge. Among them was the underworld, which, while it did not become inter-

nally stronger in the 1920s, was increased numerically by
the hordes of juvenile vagrants (*besprizorniye*) whose condition and way of life was largely a product of the Revolution, famine, and civil war.

For a long time the new regime concentrated its repressive efforts on political opponents and class aliens. Amid
the crowd of real or supposed enemies of the regime, non-
political criminals were still regarded as socially akin; they
received shorter terms of imprisonment and served them in
less severe conditions. Paradoxically, their position began
to worsen as Stalin consolidated his power, even though
Stalin, who, after all, had carried out expropriations with
the aid of common criminals, had closer links with the
underworld than any other Bolshevik leader.

The greatest danger to the underworld was not this increased severity, however, but the doctrine of social affinity.
In the twenties and thirties, common-law criminals were far
from constituting a majority of camp inmates. The regime
was conducting a campaign to change the class composition
of society, and among the millions of class aliens in the
camps were many whom the Bolsheviks wanted to get rid of
but preferred to liquidate with the aid of criminals rather
than openly. Thus political prisoners were systematically
terrorized by criminals in the camps—not, however, by all
of them—with the direct encouragement or connivance of
the authorities. The helpless politicals, unused to camp conditions, were robbed of their clothing and allowed to freeze;
their meager ration of food was taken from them, and eventually they died of exhaustion. Meanwhile they were constantly tormented and humiliated. Who can say how many
perished in Soviet camps as a direct result of this persecution
by criminals?

While the State was to blame for herding politicals and
criminals together and exposing the former to persecution,
it is clear that the criminals would have done their best,

even without official encouragement, to make the politicals'
lives unpleasant. The important point, however, is that they
did in fact collaborate with the authorities in this matter,
which was a clear violation of their traditional ethos. One
may wonder whether Stalin realized that he was not only
making use of the underworld to eliminate the class enemy
but was also gradually undermining the underworld's own
tradition by forcing or tempting it into collaboration with
the regime.

The seizure of power by amateur criminals and the
underworld's collaboration with the new regime were the
first two stages in the disruption of the underworld. The
third stage was gradual disintegration, while the master director, Stalin, prepared the way for drastic action in the
fourth. When the Nazi-Soviet war broke out, many regulars
in the camps, who were indeed the flower of the criminal
world, were given the choice of being shot or of displaying
patriotism and kinship with the regime by fighting for their
country. Thousands chose the second alternative and thus
again violated the basic law of the underworld by collab-
orating with the State authorities.

The fifth stage unfolded of itself, and the director was
able to sit back and watch events. The ex-criminals, dis-
charged from the army, returned to their previous occupation of thieving and found their way back into the prison
camps, where they discovered that the remaining guardians
of criminal morality considered them guilty of a capital
crime even though they had acted under duress. Many were
killed, but the number of scabs was unprecedented, and
there were not enough orthodox thieves to kill them all.
This started the scabs' war, which reportedly "drowned in
blood" whole areas under the camp administration. The
scabs turned the tables on their persecutors and proclaimed
a new code permitting members of the underworld to collaborate with the State in certain circumstances. Many

criminals perished in defense of the orthodox view, while many others accepted the new law. The official history of the scabs' war has not yet been written, and we do not know what role the administration played, but it is clear it hoped that the scabs would win. The orthodox code forbade thieves to perform any work in the camps, let alone perform quasi-administrative tasks, and the authorities regarded this as hampering the prisoners' reeducation. The new thieves' law permits thieves to work in labor camps and, when at liberty, to perform ordinary civic duties as a cover for their real occupation.

Since the war, the State has intensified measures against habitual criminals, and many active and respected underworld leaders have spent long periods in captivity. They are segregated from the mass of prisoners as far as possible, which makes it harder for them to keep in touch with their colleagues and with the underworld generally.

But although the State has succeeded in demoralizing the underworld and breaking down its self-isolation from society, it has not scored any appreciable success in combating crime as such. Moreover, the decline of the underworld, that is, the relaxation of its internal discipline, does not mean that it is on the brink of destruction. On the contrary, the new code makes it easier to be a thief. The underworld has adapted to the considerable changes that have occurred since the former code was established. Strictly speaking, the underworld has not declined but become more viable, and there are signs that it is very much alive. It is no less attractive than it was to large sections of the population. Many are captivated by its ideal of detachment from society and the freedom that comes from rejecting society's ethical values and prohibitions—freedom exercised, it is true, at the expense of others, but offering an outlet for deep-seated human energies, which are repressed by the official Soviet social ethic.

5

Hooliganism

At the beginning of this century, the Russian public was disturbed by violent and apparently unmotivated outbursts in the towns and in the country. The newspapers began to refer to these acts as hooliganism.* The attentive reader soon realized, however, that it was the word rather than the act that was new. Rowdyism had not increased; it was merely that the local authorities were better informed and the press had begun to report the activities of the lower classes. In 1905, the general agitation that stemmed from the anti-Government disturbances focused attention on the "new" phenomenon.

Measures against hooliganism were discussed by the Ministry of Internal Affairs, and P. P. Bashilov, the governor of Ufa province, wrote an article for the Ministry of

---

* *Izvestia* (June 13, 1973) informed its readers that the term came from an eighteenth-century nobleman named Hooligan who committed antisocial acts out of boredom. Despite this Soviet attempt to lay the blame on the aristocracy, there was, of course, no such person as Lord Hooligan. According to the philologist Ernest Weekley, quoted in *Brewer's Dictionary of Phrase and Fable*, the word was derived from a "spirited Irish family of that name whose proceedings enlivened the drab monotony of life in Southwark [South London] towards the end of the nineteenth century."

Justice in 1913 describing the phenomenon at some length.
Bashilov cited typical hooligan acts:

> Roaming the streets day and night; blaspheming and
> singing ribald songs; throwing stones at windows; tor-
> menting domestic animals; showing disrespect for
> parental, government and ecclesiastical authority; mo-
> lesting women, up to and including rape; smearing
> gates with tar; beating up passers-by and extorting
> money from them by threats; breaking into houses and
> demanding money for drink; brawling; destroying
> property by arson and other means; tearing up trees,
> shrubs, flowers, and vegetables by the roots; petty
> theft of all kinds, including that of timber stacked for
> new buildings.[1]

All these acts, Bashilov observed, were already considered crimes under the existing law, and in that sense there
was nothing new about them. Now, however, they were
being committed wantonly without any thought of personal
gain. For this reason he believed that a legal distinction
should be made between hooliganism and simple acts of
mischief committed without malice, simply to "blow off
steam," like the pranks sometimes played by young recruits
or students who had just passed an exam, or by people of
the merchant class who amused themselves by smashing
mirrors or pouring champagne into pianos. Hooliganism,
he declared, should be more severely punished than acts
like these.

Pre-Revolutionary jurists inclined to the view that while
legislation might take account of hooliganism as a social
phenomenon when fixing the penalty for illegal acts, it
should do so not by designating particular crimes as falling
within this category, but rather by recognizing hooliganism
as a motive and an aggravating circumstance in the commission of crimes already defined by the law. Otherwise the
authorities would be in the position of imposing penalties

for acts not specifically proscribed by statute. If the law declared hooliganism to be an offense in itself, it would in effect be saying that there was a crime of "misbehavior"—a term open to arbitrary interpretation by the courts—and this would have contradicted the prevailing pre-Revolutionary legal theory that criminal offenses must be strictly defined.

As might have been expected, hooliganism increased after the social convulsions of 1917. The contempt for traditional ethics instilled by the new regime, the excesses of the Civil War, and the economic difficulties that threw thousands of young people on the streets all played a part.

Children have always played at being soldiers, but the war made this type of game more popular and sometimes led to crime. According to a 1920s newspaper report, a gang of boys, the eldest of whom was sixteen, playing war, "captured" and raped a girl of six to the accompaniment of singing, shouting, and whistling (V. Vlasov, "Hooliganism in Town and Country," *Problems of Criminality*, No. 2, [Moscow, 1927]).

Vlasov lists the following types of hooligan behavior in the 1920s:

> Urinating and defecating in public, going about naked,* swearing obscenely, singing bawdy songs, molesting women, throwing snuff in people's eyes, extinguishing lights in public places, setting off false fire alarms, tearing down posters, cutting the tails off cattle, defacing monuments, breaking into mailboxes, sawing down telephone poles, smashing street lights, and drunken brawling, especially on holidays.[2]

The same author gives an interesting account of the organization of hooligan gangs. In the village of Kap-

---

* This may refer to members of the "antidecency" movement of that period, who used to parade about naked as a matter of principle.

terovskoye in northeastern Siberia there was a Central Committee of Vagabonds, which issued certificates of immunity to its members; at Durulgay near Chita on the Trans-Siberian Railroad, there was a Hooligans' League which "kept the village youth in a state of panic, robbed the poor, and terrorized the peasantry."

The frightening increase in hooliganism led to laws that expressly made it a crime. In 1922 the Criminal Code of the RSFSR defined hooliganism as "the committing of mischievous and purposeless acts accompanied by clear manifestations of disrespect for individual citizens or society in general."* This provided the courts with a convenient weapon and saved them the trouble of determining the exact article of the Code that a hooligan had violated by his acts: the term itself was sufficient to cover any not unduly serious breach of law. The maximum penalty for hooliganism in the 1922 Code was a mild one—a year's imprisonment, with or without hard labor—so that for serious offenses the courts had to apply other articles of the Code, even though public opinion might regard the case as one of hooliganism.†

It was soon apparent, however, that the 1922 definition was not broad enough. By referring to "purposeless" acts, it enabled an accused person to plead that he had not beaten up his neighbor without reason but because the neighbor had, the year before, broken his window; his conduct was,

* Hooliganism had been included in a list of crimes to be combated by Revolutionary tribunals in a decree of the Council of Peoples' Commissars, May 4, 1918, entitled "On Revolutionary Tribunals."

† In 1924 hooliganism was classed as a misdemeanor (*administrativny delikt*), with a penalty of up to three months' imprisonment for a second offense. In 1926 the maximum sentence became three months for a first offense, and two years if the acts were "committed in the course of a riot or breach of the peace, or for a second time, or persistently despite warnings by the organs of public security, or if characterized by especial blatancy [*tsinizm*] or impudence."

therefore, not hooliganism but revenge. In 1924 this gap was closed by deleting the word "purposeless" from the law. The then Commissar of Justice, Nikolai Krylenko, explained that "in the first version of our Criminal Code we spoke of 'purposeless acts,' but in the revision we have deleted this term, since clearly one cannot say that hooligan acts are committed without a purpose. If a hooligan smashes a street lamp, pulls up a curbstone, or pours a barrelful of water down a chimney, he does so purposefully: his intention is to smash the lamp or pull up the stone, and not to commit some other act."[3] For some reason even the revised definition was not broad enough for the authorities; a decree (*ukaz*) of 1940 does not define hooliganism at all, but merely lays down penalties for it.

The courts have always taken full advantage of the latitude afforded by the law, although the Supreme Court in a published decision in 1926 declared that hooliganism included "only mischievous acts involving disrespect for society which do not in themselves constitute crimes covered by other Articles of the special section of the Criminal Code."[4] This definition, however, was and still is frequently disregarded in the lower courts.

The regime's catchall legislation did not, of course, succeed in putting down hooliganism. More vigorous measures were required, and in 1925–6 a "shock campaign" was inaugurated, which increased the number of convictions sevenfold.[5] In February 1927, the Commissariat of Justice[6] instructed local executive committees to issue rules for combating hooliganism, as indeed they had already been doing. In December 1925, for example, a district committee in the Crimean town of Simferopol had issued a regulation to combat hooliganism and drunkenness which, after prohibiting public disturbances and prescribing rules for the sale of strong drink, forbade the public to "assemble on sidewalks without a specific purpose or to sit on the window sills of houses and shops."[7] I have quoted this not for comic relief but because it illustrates the touching belief of the "workers, peasants, and Red Army deputies," newly installed in the seats of power, that deep-seated social evils could be cured by removing their symptoms, rather than by uncovering and facing up to their causes—which the authorities were not always willing to do.* It was not long, indeed, before the regime gave up any attempt to investigate the causes of crime and concentrated on tightening up the penalties.† In 1935 the penalty for hooliganism was increased to five years' imprisonment, and the courts were severely criticized for not having handed down more sentences for this crime the previous year. Stalin's thesis that the class struggle became more acute as the building of socialism progressed was used not only as a weapon against politicals: in 1936 the journal *Soviet Justice* declared that the reason hooliganism had run riot was the intensification of the class struggle.[9]

The law in force at present in the Soviet Union defines hooliganism as "intentional acts which seriously disturb

---

* According to Mikhail Tomsky, chairman of the Trade Union Council, a similar ordinance in Vladimir province forbade, among other things, "brawling and excessive noise; shouting, singing, and music on streets and in private houses after 10 P.M.; throwing explosive devices in public places; using firearms and toy pistols; discharging such weapons in inhabited sections or places of assembly, except in self-defense; committing acts of impropriety in public, e.g., approaching bathers of the opposite sex; using obscene and abusive language in public; committing acts of hooliganism against individual citizens or molesting them in public; deliberately jostling passers-by or striking them with switches; walking along the sidewalk in large groups and obstructing passers-by, splashing them with water, mud, or spittle, throwing snow at them; casting stones or other objects at passing animals."[8]

† The science of criminology had been practically abandoned in the USSR by the end of the 1920s. After Stalin's death, jurists began to investigate the sociology of crime again, but their efforts were hampered by ideological restraints, the lack of published statistics on crime, and other restrictions.

public order and show clear disrespect for society,"[10] a definition as broad as that of 1924. The same law defines "malicious hooliganism" as "the same acts committed in an especially impudent or blatant manner"—literally "with exceptional blatancy [*tsinizm*] or especial impudence." Since neither impudence nor blatancy is defined, a wide margin of interpretation is left to the courts.* This classification is crucial because simple hooliganism is punishable by up to one year's imprisonment, and malicious hooliganism (without the use of weapons) by up to five.

The flexibility of the definition is probably intentional, however. It has long been Soviet practice to draft laws in such general terms that as many offenders as possible can be pulled in.† But the vagueness of the antihooligan law is extreme even by Soviet standards. This is not necessarily a hindrance in the campaign against hooliganism, but it does put the courts in danger of either stretching the law or failing to use it to the full. For example, the Stavropol regional court in 1967 convicted a defendant, B., of simple hooliganism, stating that his action was not blatant or impudent. A Soviet jurist criticized this verdict,[13] arguing that even simple hooliganism was, as a rule, blatant and impudent, but that B.'s acts did not involve *especial* blatancy and impudence. He continued: "Especial blatancy connotes *behavior* toward others which completely disregards the norms of morality and propriety, such as relieving oneself

* The law specifies other detailed criteria, which I will not discuss here. The maximum penalty for hooliganism, involving the use or attempted use of weapons, is seven years' imprisonment.

† The law against hooliganism is also used for political cases. In 1969 Sergei Sarychev[11] was convicted of hooliganism for expressing anti-Soviet views in a restaurant, and A. M. Zemtsov[12] in 1970 for damaging a photograph of Stalin on public display in Leningrad. As will be discussed in the next chapter, radio hams who broadcast without permission are also classed as hooligans.

in public.* Especial impudence is a question of the subject's *attitude* toward people, toward the community and its rules." As an example of especial impudence he cited the following story:

> A. came home drunk at two in the morning and banged at the door. As it was not opened at once, he smashed the panel with a log, broke into the room, and started to wreck it. He overturned the bed on which his sister and her husband were sleeping, beat his sister, cut the electric wiring, smashed the crockery, knocked over the stove, threw bricks in all directions and fired two rifle shots at the ceiling. These actions were quite properly regarded as especially impudent, and the defending lawyer's argument to the contrary was without foundation.[14]

It would be interesting to know what form the lawyer's argument took, or what criteria are valid in cases of this sort. What, for instance, is the basis for the statement in *Commentary to the RSFSR Criminal Code* (1971) that if a hooligan pushes someone or grabs him by the coattails, his is not a case of "especial blatancy or impudence"?

---

* The Soviet criminologist A. A. Gertsenzon (*Criminal Law and Sociology* [Moscow, 1970]) mentions three cases in which men received two-year sentences for urinating in public when drunk and suggests that this was excessive: "It would have been better to fine them 25 or 50 rubles each, and bring the matter to public notice." (This seems a little odd, since the men were punished precisely for the publicity of their action.) Gertsenzon does not relate the circumstances, but I suspect that, as in many such cases, the men felt an urgent need when there was no public toilet around and took advantage of a doorway. This is a common custom in Russia and accounts for the appalling smell in many doorways, especially in houses situated near taverns.

There are, of course, also cases where people deliberately urinate or defecate in public, sometimes accompanying their action by bad language or what Soviet courts call obscene (*tsinichny*) gestures. These, however, obviously come under the heading of blatancy, and presumably the cases referred to by Gertsenzon were not of this aggravated kind, or he would not have recommended that a fine be substituted for imprisonment.

The same jurist[15] admits that it is hard to distinguish precisely between "exceptional blatancy" and "especial impudence," but gives an instance to which both these criteria apply:

A., while drunk, began to molest in hooligan fashion [literally "from hooligan motives"] M., who was bathing in the sea, and attempted to pull off her swimming clothes. When she went to the beach he continued to molest her, using obscene language, kicks and blows, until prevented by members of the public and police.

Here, on the other hand, is a case in which the Supreme Court[16] decided that "exceptional blatancy or impudence" did *not* apply:

Ukladov, when drunk, tried to enter a restaurant, but the doorman refused to take his coat and asked him to leave. After a time he returned, went up to the doorman and pulled his cap over his eyes, after which he hit another doorman in the face. The doorman overpowered him, and he used obscene language in the restaurant lobby.

The Gorky city court brought in a verdict of malicious hooliganism, but the Supreme Court reversed it, declaring that Ukladov's conduct was not marked by exceptional blatancy or impudence.

In studying reports of hooliganism the variety of offenses involved is striking: obscene abuse in public, quarrels with neighbors in communal apartments,* brawls in restaurants

---

* In communal apartments, several families share bath, toilet, and kitchen facilities. According to Gertsenzon, every third case of malicious hooliganism occurs in a communal apartment,[17] and one-quarter of hooligans' victims are their wives. Systematic wife-beating is often punished not as hooliganism but as torture (*istyazanie*)—Article 113 of the Code.

Andrei Amalrik in his book *Involuntary Journey to Siberia* (New York, 1970), pp. 74, 262, has said that close to half of the men convicted of hooliganism are brought to justice by their wives. Wives frequently complain to the police that their husbands beat them, and Amalrik quotes

or on the street, drunken gangs breaking into a club or a Red Corner (recreation room); wife-beating, cursing the neighbors when they come to comfort her, breaking up property, smashing glasses—all without any sign of the motives that usually lead to crime.

It is often hard to understand why a man suddenly goes berserk and apparently "blows off steam" by attacking the first person or thing that crosses his path. Here is an example of such a case.

> On the evening of November 4, 1965, Tenyukh, who was drunk, attempted in the presence of his children to beat his wife. He chased her when she tried to hide with the neighbors, drove the children away, cut up and tore to pieces clothes, sheets, and blankets, threw ripped-up pillows into the street, broke a mirror and a lampshade, tore out the electric wiring, and threw bottles and saucepans full of food into the corridor. Returning to the room he lit matches and boasted to the other inmates of the apartment that he would set fire to it. In this way he disturbed their normal repose.[18]

Hooliganism and vandalism are closely allied, but the vandal who creates less commotion than the rowdy hooligan is prosecuted under different articles, which cover destruction of personal or State property, even though his motivation may be much the same. Common acts of vandalism in the Soviet Union are breaking street lamps and windows, throwing stones at passing trains, putting pub-

---

a prosecutor who tried to persuade a village meeting that such complaints should be made less often: "What happens is that some woman accuses her husband of beating her. He gets a three-year sentence, and a month later she comes along and says: 'Let him go, please. I've forgiven him.' So next time just you think twice before denouncing your husbands because once we put someone in jail we don't let him go till he has served his sentence."

lic telephones out of order, and desecrating tombstones. Smashed-up monuments are a common sight in Russian cemeteries. Vandals are particularly fond of using the glassed-over photographs of the deceased as targets for stone-throwing.*

Acts of vandalism are often impulsively committed by groups of young men, and they frequently contain an element of curiosity as well as destructiveness. At Archangel some youths boarded a self-propelled barge in the harbor and took the pilot house to pieces, walking off with the instruments and engine parts, which they finally threw away.[19]

Acts of hooliganism may be coolly calculated in advance, even when they appear senseless. "Zlatin suggested to some youths that they should beat up the first man they happened to meet. When a man came along, Zlatin told them to go ahead, and they knocked the man down and started to beat him."† (*Bulletin of the RSFSR Supreme Court*, 1963).

Hooliganism may, in some cases, be due to neither a morbid impulse nor malice, but rather to a spirit of mischief that can even be good-natured. Mischief, good-natured or not, was traditional among the Russian peasantry, like their customs of daubing tar on the gate of a house inhabited by a new bride of doubtful reputation.[20]

Bashilov[21] wrote in 1913 with disapproval of the "immoral practice, still not eradicated from our schools, of 'hazing' new boys, that is to say mocking, and even beating

---

* This is no new practice in Russia: "A group of young people, including senior schoolboys, went for a walk in the cemetery of a large provincial town and threw stones at the sculpted angels and saints; they were delighted when a nose or an ear was knocked off by a lucky shot" (Gromov, "Motiveless Crime," *Journal of the Ministry of Justice*, 1913).

† I strongly suspect that this was actually an instance of training fledgling criminals.

and torturing, a new pupil simply because he is new, though he has done none of his comrades any harm. The insults, ill-treatment, and violence to which new boys are subjected deserves no other name than hooliganism."

A common Russian prank in hostels and hospitals is to roll up a piece of paper, stick it between the toes of a sleeping comrade and set fire to it; the victim's panic on awakening is greeted with roars of laughter. (Once, in the 1930s, this trick misfired. The victim was badly burnt and turned out to be a Stakhanovite, or special worker, who took a poor view of such games. The perpetrators were punished for sabotaging the Stakhanovite movement.)[22]

As we have seen, Soviet law originally defined hooliganism as purposeless acts but later dropped this qualification. Many hooligan acts today seem pointless in the ordinary sense, but others are clearly prompted by motives like jealousy or revenge. For example, a woman was convicted of hooliganism for obscenely insulting another woman of whom she was jealous, breaking her windows with stones, and on the following day, pulling her hair in the house manager's office and hitting her several times on the head with a shopping bag.[23]

Another convicted hooligan, one Gusev, quarreled with his mother-in-law Kleshcheva because she would not tell him where his wife and child were hiding. He came to her apartment, smashed a cupboard, a baby carriage, and a glass pitcher, threw other objects about and went away. That evening he poured kerosene over the apartment door and the landing and set fire to it. According to a witness, he then ran down the street waving his arms in the air, using obscene language and shouting that his mother-in-law's place was on fire. The Supreme Court judgment ran in part: "The witness Ovchinnikov, a member of the regular police force, states that on August 30, 1961, Gusev came into the police station and said he had set fire to his mother-in-law's home. Gusev's behavior shows that his act was one of hooliganism, but does not indicate that he intended to cause Kleshcheva's death."[24]

According to the criminologist Alexei A. Gertsenzon,[25] 42 percent of the acts defined by the courts as malicious hooliganism consist of beating and bodily injuries. And Filanovsky[26] attributes 61 percent of the hooliganism committed by minors to actions of this kind. For example, a man named Yudin was convicted by a lower court of hooliganism after he had beaten another man named Osipov and his wife. When the case went to the Supreme Court it was found that Osipov's wife had begun the fight by hitting Yudin over the head with a bucket, and that the origin of the quarrel lay in Yudin's and Osipov's relations at work. The Supreme Court therefore held that Yudin was motivated not by hooliganism but by his unfriendly relations with Osipov. Yudin's action was defined as the infliction of minor bodily harm, and his punishment was correspondingly reduced.

As to Yudin's behavior (he had cursed at Osipov), the Court observed that "the use of obscene language is a feature of petty hooliganism,"[27] which indeed was stated in the decree of 1966 that increased the penalties for petty hooliganism.[28] Swearing is an extremely common offense in Russia, though it is evidently considered reprehensible by the law. Incidentally, the word used for "obscene"— netsenzurny—means literally "unacceptable to the censorship [tsenzura]." It is fortunate that obscenity is considered only petty hooliganism, which means that it falls within the domain of administrative rather than criminal sanctions; otherwise the danger of mass repressions would be great. As it is, if a person has already been punished for petty hooliganism, repetition of the offense within twelve months is treated as a criminal offense.*

If a man persists in using obscene language on a particu-

---

* According to Gertsenzon,[29] abuse and insults account for 37 percent of all acts defined by the courts as malicious hooliganism.

lar occasion, this, too, may be treated as a criminal offense. The following such case is taken from a decision of the RSFSR Supreme Court.

> On October 15, 1962, Tarasov, being drunk, entered the courtyard of No. 18, Sibirskaya Street, Astrakhan, and there used obscene language in the presence of other citizens. He continued to do so as they were turning him out of the yard. Some time later he returned and knocked several times at the door of the apartment of Citizeness Maltseva, still using obscene language.[30]

Of course, not everyone who uses obscene language is dealt with under administrative procedure—for one thing this would be physically impossible. From time to time a man is arrested if a policeman happens to be near by, or if his language is too outrageous. When he gets to the police station, the air is blue with obscenity anyway; the lower ranks of the army and police, like many other sections of the population, use expressions of the "motherfucking" type more or less as interjections, without paying attention to their meaning. So, incidentally, do officers, even when they are giving orders. When the offender is pushed into a cell, things are no different; nor are they for that matter on the shop floor, or in drawing rooms frequented by intellectuals.

This is not to say that everyone in Russia talks obscenely on all occasions. In some circles it is not done in front of women and children. On the whole, however, most people use obscene language and at the same time find it quite natural that obscenity should be a punishable offense.* This

---

* This was not always so, however. A pre-Revolutionary proverb makes light of abusive language ("Hard words don't stick to your collar"), and in the 1920s the Soviet author Orshansky[31] observed that people were surprised that foul language was treated as a crime. "Swearing is deeply ingrained in the masses' way of life and mentality, and they simply cannot understand that something so elementary as 'using language' should be punished by the courts."

sounds paradoxical, but it is a piece of social hypocrisy that must be recognized. To all appearances, this sort of hypocrisy is even more widespread than the tendency to praise political decisions by the government with which one does not in fact agree. I should make clear that I am speaking here of public prosecutions for obscene language, not of civil suits initiated by the target of such insults. In the latter case, it is understandable that the insulted person feels aggrieved, but in the former case the aggrieved party is, supposedly, the State or society as a whole. This suggests that obscene words are regarded as having mystic significance and power, and anyone who resorts to this form of sorcery in public is presumed to be an enemy of society.

Hooliganism can also be practiced by correspondence. Thus we read[32] in G. S. Sarkisov's *The Prevention of Violations of the Public Order* (Yerevan, 1972) that a convicted hooligan addressed dozens of communications full of obscene and insulting terms to "highly placed authorities of the Party, the judiciary, and the public prosecutor's office" in the hope that many people would read them and suffer moral detriment. The charge in this case was malicious hooliganism. I do not know of any prosecutions for writing letters of this sort without obscene language in them, but I imagine it would be possible, especially since persons who believe their rights have been violated tend to express themselves in no uncertain terms.

The social status of persons convicted of hooliganism varies in different parts of the Soviet Union. To judge from the study by G. S. Sarkisov, an Armenian jurist, Armenian hooligans apparently come from all sections of the population, and their educational level, while lower than average, is higher than one might have expected: 22 percent had completed secondary education, and 7.5 percent were university students or graduates. According to the results of an investigation made by the All-Union Institute for the Study

of the Causes and the Prevention of Crime,* which Sarkisov cites, nearly half the workers convicted of hooliganism had a perfunctory or indifferent attitude to their work,
most were untrained or semiskilled; only 23.5 percent took
part in group activities, and then without enthusiasm.

Sarkisov also presents the results of a character analysis
of Armenian hooligans convicted between 1966 and 1968.
This study is interesting not so much because of its statistics
as because of the ideological preconceptions revealed in the
definition of positive and negative character traits. The lack
of control groups and of any explanation of the statistical
methods used are typical of the primitive nature of current
Soviet sociological research.

Psychological traits (good/bad)	Percentage of those consistently displaying the traits in question in various situations and activities	
	Good	Bad
Steadfastness/lack of principle	30.0	35.0
Collectivism/individualism	11.8	35.3
Flexibility/obstinacy	18.0	35.3
Sociability/aloofness	30.0	9.0
Frankness/secretiveness	30.0	6.0
Kindness, gentleness/malice, cruelty	16.0	35.0
Generosity/greed	35.3	18.0
Disinterestedness/self-interest	18.0	11.8
Respectfulness/lack of respect	6.0	58.0

Note: In the remaining cases these traits were not clearly displayed.

Most of the hooligans investigated did not have hobbies
or spare-time interests such as sports or the arts. None of
them painted, collected stamps, or bred tropical fish, but
most of them were fond of open-air dancing, picnics, etc.

* The All-Union Institute for the Study of the Causes and the Prevention of Crime was established in 1963 under the Procurator's Office
of the USSR. This institute undertakes research and publications in the
field of criminology and trains criminologists.

Sarkisov draws the conclusion that hooligans are people of poor education and few interests, but, as is usual in Soviet criminological publications, he does not give any data for the control group. He states further that in 80 percent of the cases of hooliganism, the perpetrator was drunk; this correlation is confirmed by other sources.

It is hard to find in the works of Soviet criminologists any more precise details from which a picture of the criminal's psychology could be drawn. However, Gertsenzon gives a fairly extensive account of a convicted hooligan.

V., aged eighteen, was sentenced to five years' imprisonment on the charge that he and his companions entered the Red Corner of a hostel where a dance was in progress and committed acts of hooliganism, breaking doors, overturning tables, stools, and chairs and attacking girls who were dancing. They also attacked the policemen who arrested them. The incident took place at 7 P.M. on a Saturday. V. and his companions were drunk at the time, as V. had been celebrating the receipt of his first driver's license.

V. was born in July 1937, the son of an electrician employed in an industrial enterprise at Yaroslavl, a city on the upper Volga. He lived with his father, mother, elder sister, and grandmother. His father often came home drunk and beat his wife in front of the children, for which he was sentenced to one month's imprisonment under Article 146 of the 1926 Criminal Code. One night, when he was very drunk, he tried to enter a guarded building site. After several warnings, the sentry fired, and the father was killed.

V. was ashamed of his father and especially of the circumstances of his death. His mother had her aged mother and two small children to support. During the war years they lived in Yaroslavl in an impoverished condition.

Up to his seventh year of school V. was a conscientious student but after that he began to play truant. He was kept back for a year because of his poor progress, but continued to neglect his studies and finally dropped out of school.

Soon afterwards he took a job in the Severokhod factory as an unskilled worker, soling shoes and boots. All his family worked except the grandmother. Their total wages were 175 rubles (roughly $200) a month —his mother earned 60, his sister 40, and V. himself 75. After two years he left the factory to train to be a truck driver, but he was arrested on the present charge immediately after receiving his license.

Prior to his arrest, the family of four lived in a room measuring nine square meters, sharing kitchen, bath, and toilet facilities with their neighbors, in a house in the center of the city, close to a theater and two movie houses. In his spare time V. went to the movies, the park, and open-air dances. He went to the "live" theater only three times, while he was still at school. He hardly ever read books. He often drank with friends, especially on payday.

His home life was happy, and his mother and sister are much grieved by his arrest.

V. stated in conversation that he began to drink vodka at the age of fourteen or fifteen, while he was in school, and drank more heavily after he started work at the factory. Out of his monthly wage of 75 rubles* he gave his mother 20 for board and spent the rest as he pleased, mostly on drink.

In reply to questioning, his family, neighbors, and the house manager stated that V. was frequently drunk at home and in public. He was pulled in several times by the police for hooligan acts and on three occasions was placed in the drunk tank to sober up.

Questioning at his place of work established that

* Although the date of the report is 1956, the figure is apparently adjusted to the 1961 currency reform. After taxes, V.'s remaining monthly wage would have bought about twenty-five pint bottles of vodka or fifty-five pounds of butter.

conditions were normal in his shop, he was a conscientious worker and received no reprimands. He did not make friends with other workers or join in factory activities. Neither the factory administration nor the factory social organizations knew anything about his life outside the factory.

At the time he was interviewed, V. had served ten months of his sentence. The administration of the corrective labor colony stated that he was assigned to general labor duties, worked well and obeyed the regulations. During this period he had qualified as a sewing-machine adjuster.

From the interview it appeared that he read newspapers, listened to the radio, and was conversant with international and domestic affairs. He felt remorse for his crime and concern about what his friends would think. The court session that tried him had been held in the Red Corner where he committed the offense; he was mortified by this, as many of his friends and acquaintances were present. Asked what had made him commit the crime, he said that no one had prompted him to do it, but that he had lost his self-control and his faith in himself.[33]

Soviet jurists hold different views about what motivates hooliganism. Some speak of hooligan impulses, others of a too lively sense of mischief, while still others deny that there is a single motive. I. G. Filanovsky, quoting a study of juvenile hooliganism in Leningrad in 1970, says that 29 percent of cases studied were due to mischief, 8 percent to a misguided sense of comradeship, and 1 percent to "false romanticism"; while in some cases proceedings provided no indication whatever of the motive. It is hard to know how Soviet writers arrive at these findings. In one case, we are told that a student in a workers' school turned up in a drunken condition, disrupted lessons, brandished a screwdriver, and threatened a female teacher's life; when asked afterwards why he had done it, he replied, "I wanted to gain prestige by showing the others how strong and fearless I was."[34] This may have been his motive, but I suspect that his choice of words owed something to prompting by the interviewer, the public prosecutor, or some other person. In cases like this, when Soviet jurists quote criminals' accounts of their motives, one generally has the feeling that the subjects have been coached, or else that they know what answer is expected of them and the language to use.

In the early days of the Soviet regime a legal principle that was extensively applied in criminal law was what might be called guilt by analogy. It was spelled out in the 1926 Criminal Code:

> Where a socially dangerous act has not been expressly dealt with in the present Code, the basis and limits of responsibility for it shall be determined in conformity with those Articles of the Code which deal with the crimes most closely resembling it.

The same principle figured in pre-Revolutionary jurisprudence. Article 151 of the Criminal and Correctional Code of 1885 read:

> If no punishment is provided by law for a criminal act of which the accused is found guilty, the court shall impose the sentence laid down for one of the crimes that, by their nature and circumstances, are most similar to the act in question.

This article seems to have been applied cautiously, but sometimes curiously. After studying a number of actual cases, N. S. Tagantsev concluded in 1912 as follows:

> Article 1476, dealing with parents whose cruel treatment drives their children to suicide, can be applied to cases where the parents unintentionally provoke them to any other crime.

Article 1477, on mutilation, can be applied to the act of piercing a child's hymen with one's finger.

The Articles dealing with homosexuality can be applied to unnatural copulation with a woman, as the essential feature of the crime is the way in which carnal passion is satisfied, and not the sex of the person with whom it is satisfied.[35]

Under the 1926 Code, analogy was applied more widely, and courts and administrative organs freely decided which actions were punishable by analogy with which articles. This went so far that in 1937 Andrei Vyshinsky, who was then Chief Public Prosecutor, accused the courts of being overenthusiastic. "Judicial practice has shown that the principle of analogy is often resorted to in cases where courts consider that the existing articles of the Criminal Code do not provide for sufficiently severe punishments. In order to remedy this they sometimes go out of their way to invoke a different article, even though there is already an article covering the act in question."*

In 1926 two youths in the Ukraine were convicted of rape by analogy: angry at a girl who had refused to have sexual relations with them, they caught her in a secluded place and pierced her hymen with a nail, but did not have intercourse with her.[36]

In 1937, in the Orenburg district, a man named Dominov was convicted by a People's Court of inflicting grievous bodily harm because he had performed the rite of circumcision. The District Court, on appeal, "corrected" the verdict and defined the crime as analogous to abortion.†

At present Soviet law excludes the principle of analogy, by Articles 3 and 7 of the Fundamental Principles of Crim-

* *Soviet Justice* (1937), No. 2, p. 3.
† This case was quoted in an article in *Soviet Justice* (1937), Nos. 23–24, by K. Tavgazov who argued, very boldly for that time, that the principle of analogy was contrary to the Constitution of the USSR.

inal Legislation. Article 3 states that only "socially dangerous acts provided for by law" entail criminal responsibility. The law does not, however, indicate how specific the reference in the Criminal Code must be, and the definitions of various punishable acts are so broad that there is plenty of room for the use of analogy in practice.

One of the most conveniently vague definitions is that of hooliganism—"intentional acts seriously violating public order and expressing clear disrespect for society." Any crime, especially an intentional one, is a serious disturbance of public order. To complicate the matter further, Soviet law is not at all clear about what it means by "public order," and an act need not be a crime to be considered an offense on this basis. In a 1968 case,[37] a religious procession in a forest was held to be a disturbance of public order. This seemed to contradict earlier criticism by zealous atheists of that article of the Criminal Code which makes it a criminal offense to obstruct religious rites insofar as they do not violate public order (Article 143 of the present Criminal Code). Plakshin, a Soviet lawyer, wrote indignantly in 1924 that Soviet officials risked prosecution if they tried to stop a religious procession "anywhere outside of a village, where public order would not be disturbed." Since then, the term "public order" has obviously widened its scope.

"Open disrespect for society" can also be regarded as a generic characteristic of any sort of crime, especially in the sense in which it is used in Soviet courts. *The Course of Soviet Criminal Law*, a six-volume Soviet textbook edited by prominent lawyers and published in 1971, states: "If a lone passer-by is attacked late at night by a drunken hooligan, the open disrespect for society consists in the fact that any member of society might have been the victim; the criminal had no personal motive but attacked a complete stranger at random."

This view is discussed at length, including the fact that it still applies even if a man murders someone for personal reasons, since any other member of society *might* have been the object of the animosity that led to the murder.

Thus, almost any crime or supposedly antisocial act may be classified as hooliganism, which is a great boon to the courts when they think an act ought to be punished but cannot find an article of the Code to fit it.

A flagrant example of how the principle of analogy is used for what are not crimes under the law but simple misdemeanors is the prosecution of radio hams or, as they are called in the Soviet Union, radio hooligans.

Radio transmitters in the USSR must be licensed.* A 1960[38] law specifies administrative (as opposed to criminal) penalties for "constructing or using radio transmitters without due permission." The punishment for a first offense is a 50-ruble fine and confiscation of the apparatus; for a second, the fine is trebled. According to the act, evidence of violation must be considered by a People's Court within three days of its being furnished by the police, in the presence of the offender and any necessary witnesses.

This has, however, proved to be the kind of offense for which, as Vyshinsky put it, the courts have found the law insufficiently severe. While lower courts are not, at the present time, supposed to apply the principle of analogy, its

---

* Soon after the Revolution, the private use of radio sets was forbidden by Article 23 of the RSFSR Civil Code (1922). Then, in 1924, private persons and organizations were permitted to install and operate receiving sets "in order to promote radio communication and the radio industry and to improve knowledge of radio techniques."[39] They were allowed to receive public broadcasts, broadcasts in Morse code, weather bulletins, and time signals, but not foreign broadcasts. All operators had to be registered, and under Article 191 of the 1926 Criminal Code, a fine was imposed for operating a receiving station without a license or violating its conditions. Special permission was required for operating a receiving station in a frontier zone.[40] When war broke out in 1941, all receivers were requisitioned, and it became a criminal offense to conceal one. The license system for receivers was abolished in the 1950s.

use was tacitly prescribed, in 1963, by a plenary session of the Supreme Court of the USSR,[41] which stated that "intentional acts taking the form of radio transmissions involving open disrespect for society, carried out with mischievous intent, gravely disturbing public order, or interfering with broadcasting and official radio communications," were to be considered, according to circumstances, as either hooliganism or malicious hooliganism. If, the statement rather mysteriously continued, transmitters were used in the commission of some other crime, this crime should be punished in the same way as if radio apparatus had not been used. Apparently, what is meant here is spreading information unpalatable to the regime, which is classified as anti-Soviet agitation or "dissemination of fabrications discrediting the Soviet system."

Although the Supreme Court did not specifically mention the principle of analogy, the ruling clearly implies it: it does not say that the acts in question actually are hooliganism, but that they are to be considered as such. Moreover, the wording differs from that of the law in suggesting that "disrespect for society" and "disturbance of public order" are independent criteria, either of which makes an act criminal, and in introducing a third criterion, "mischievous intent." If unauthorized broadcasts interfere with official communications, then according to the Court's ruling, they amount to hooliganism even if the criteria of "disrespect for society" and "disturbance of public order" are not present.

The fact that the plenum of the Supreme Court directed judges' attention to the "increased social danger of these crimes" suggests that unauthorized ham operators must have been quite numerous in 1963; and their number may have increased since then. At any rate, the Soviet press, especially in the provinces, has devoted a good deal of attention to radio hooligans. The articles give the impression that many of the broadcasts are harmless musical programs, though the music is of the type—jazz or rock—frowned on by Soviet officialdom; the broadcasts also include jokes and, according to some reports, bad language. The press emphasizes the alleged interference with official broadcasting, but, as the court ruling shows, this is not the only reason for persecuting ham operators.

It is hard to predict the authorities' reaction to the fact that more and more young people are learning how to construct low-power transmitters,* whether they will make it easier for them to obtain licenses or intensify repressive measures.

---

* The technique of locating the source of radio transmissions is well developed in the USSR, and it is no doubt simple to trace a moderately strong amateur transmitter; but low-power transmitters can be moved from place to place easily and are, therefore, harder to find.

6

Murder

In the Soviet Union as elsewhere, most murders are committed by people who have not killed before and who are led to do so by some acute personal or social conflict. Not enough information has been published to analyze the most frequent causes of such conflicts in the USSR with any degree of accuracy, but frequently the victims are relatives or spouses, both legal and common-law.*

Intentional homicide is punished in the Soviet Union by deprivation of freedom for a term of three to ten years (Article 103 of the RSFSR Criminal Code). Homicide under aggravating circumstances (specified as: from mercenary motives; from motives of hooliganism; committed in

---

* According to Gertsenzon's selective analysis of 100 cases, domestic categories accounted for 42 percent of the victims of premeditated murder. In my own files, comprising 300 cases of murder for ascertained motives committed during the period 1961–1975, they represent only 25 percent. However, my files are based only on published information about criminal cases.

According to S. V. Borodin,[1] in a selected region, 24 percent of the victims were wives, 10.5 percent common-law wives, 22 percent relatives, 31.5 percent neighbors and acquaintances, and 12 percent fellow workers. Borodin comments: "Thus the motivation of these crimes generally stems from everyday life." (S. V. Borodin, *Judicial Procedure in Murder Trials*, [Moscow, 1964]).

connection with the victim's performance of his official or social duty; committed with special cruelty; committed in a manner dangerous for the life of many persons; in conjunction with rape; of a woman known by the guilty person to be pregnant; of two or more persons; committed by a person who has already committed intentional homicide; committed because of a blood feud; or committed by an especially dangerous recidivist) is punished by deprivation of freedom for a term of eight to fifteen years with or without subsequent exile, or by death (Article 102 of the RSFSR Criminal Code).

Intentional homicide committed in a state of sudden strong mental agitation provoked by force or grave insult on the part of the victim, or provoked by other unlawful actions of the victim is punished by deprivation of freedom for a term not exceeding five years or by correctional labor (without deprivation of freedom) for a term not exceeding one year (Article 104 of the RSFSR Criminal Code).

V. N. Kudryavtsev[2] remarked in his book *Motivation in Criminology* (Moscow, 1968) that in over 80 percent of the murders of spouses there is a background of domestic trouble. (Presumably in the other 20 percent the murder took place inadvertently in an atmosphere of domestic bliss.) In some reported cases the motive was to get rid of a wife in order to marry or live with another woman or to punish her for trying to leave home. In one case cited by Borodin, a man who had served sentences for murdering two previous wives attempted to murder his third by shooting her and then throwing her in a pit filled with water; he was convicted and sentenced to death. The reason for his wife-murdering propensity is not stated.

Murders of husbands by wives are generally motivated by ill-treatment. In another case reported by Borodin, the husband used to make fun of his wife and on one occasion declared he was not the father of the child she was carrying.

She grabbed an ax and hit him over the head several times. The local court ruled that the insult was not a grave one and convicted her of murder for revenge. The Supreme Court, however, found that the murder was committed in a state of sudden and violent mental agitation, which is a mitigating circumstance.

Family disputes are often caused by the husband's habitual drunkenness, especially when the household is badly off. A woman named Chauzova was convicted of murdering her husband after she found him in a drunken sleep by the bank of a river without either the money he had been paid that day or his wrist watch. She killed him by hitting him several times on the head with a stick.*

In classic cases where a husband commits murder when he comes home and finds his wife in bed with a lover, the courts have sometimes ruled that he acted on an emotional impulse inspired by a "grave affront to his marital feelings,"[3] and considered it a mitigating circumstance. Formerly, in the 1920s and 1930s, Soviet jurists regarded jealousy as a "base motive" and an aggravation of the crime.

The murder of a common-law wife is often prompted by the desire to get rid of her or to punish her for wanting to break off relations. It may also be connected with her pregnancy. For instance, Borodin reports that a man killed his mistress when she told him she was pregnant in order to persuade him to leave his wife. Fearing trouble at home and at work, he lured her into the forest and killed her. An autopsy showed that she was not pregnant, but despite this he was sentenced for the murder of a pregnant woman.

A kept woman may kill her lover out of jealousy or in revenge for unfaithfulness, or she may kill her rival. An unusual case was a woman named P., aged seventy-four, who lived on a farm in the Rostov region. Despite her ad-

* Reported in the *Bulletin of the RSFSR Supreme Court*, 1962, no. 6.

vanced age she had several lovers and was in the habit of entertaining strangers and drinking with them. A lodger, aged twenty-five, developed an attachment for her which aroused the jealousy of his twenty-two-year-old mistress, who eventually killed her aged rival with an ax.[4]

Family troubles can lead to the murder of parents. Peter D. killed his father with an ax because he had mocked him;[5] B., aged sixteen, killed his father because, when drunk, he used to beat up his wife.[6] Aged parents who become a burden in difficult economic or housing conditions are sometimes murdered. A woman named R., convicted of killing her mother, said the latter had been ill for over a year; she had gotten tired of constantly looking after her, and the hospital would not take her in. Furthermore, her long illness had been a cause of discord in the family.[7]

In other cases, parents may be the victims of refined, "motiveless" cruelty. S. told his mother that he intended to kill her; she cried out, "No, no, I want to die a natural death!" Whereupon he took a kitchen knife, cut the veins in her arm, and prevented her from stanching the wounds, so that she died.[8]

The traditional motive for killing relatives, to inherit from them, is, I imagine, less prevalent in Russia than it was. It might have been supposed that the Soviet regime did away with this cause of crime once and for all when, in May 1918, it abolished the right of inheritance with a few exceptions. But as Petr Stuchka, first Bolshevik Commissar of Justice and editor of the *Encyclopedia of State and Law* (Moscow, 1925–27), observes, "The decree had no special economic results at the time; there was no power to enforce it in the general disorder." In 1922, the Civil Code reestablished the right of inheritance, and from 1926 on there has been no limit to the amount which may be inherited.

Domestic murders are often the result of a drunken quarrel, especially during some family festivity. In a case cited by Podbegaylo in 1965, a man who was being entertained by relatives picked a quarrel with them for not coming to his name-day party;[9] in a case cited by Borodin in 1964, two brothers quarreled over which of them paid more frequent visits to the grave of their mother, who had recently died.[10] Both these cases ended in murder.

In the Soviet press and in Soviet studies of crime it is often pointed out that family conflicts ending in murder are usually the culmination of a long period of ill-feeling, during which the police have received warnings of intended murder but have not acted on them. This is not necessarily a reflection on the police. Threats of murder are frequently made in family circles and elsewhere; they are in themselves a criminal offense in Russia, but it would be physically impossible to prosecute everyone who makes such a threat in the heat of a quarrel.

Brawls not in the family circle but occasioned by some serious social conflict, the nature of which is seldom clear from published reports, are also the motive of many murders. I have already cited Segalov's study[11] of village conflicts in the 1920s, when bloody brawls resulted from seemingly insignificant causes. Even today village celebrations often end in violent drunken quarrels. Soviet authors are fond of pointing out that most of these quarrels occur on religious holidays, but as far as I can judge, religion has nothing to do with it: the same brawls take place at weddings and on Revolutionary holidays.* The subject is so little studied that contemporary writers do not even men-

---

* Gertsenzon[12] in his *Introduction to Soviet Criminology* (Moscow, 1965) states that 13 percent of all murders are committed on "State holidays" and 21 percent on religious ones. I would point out that there are only eight State holidays in the year, while the religious holidays are far more numerous. (No religious holidays are officially celebrated in the USSR, but Easter and other traditional holidays are privately observed.)

tion the survivals of a blood feud system (recorded by Segalov) among the Russian peasantry.

It is easier to understand the social conflicts that arise between country people and the students or employees from the town who are brought to help with the harvest and other agricultural tasks. The townspeople have to live in unfamiliar conditions, doing work they are not used to and often do not want to do; many of them are depressed and find solace only in drink. The villagers believe, not without reason, that people have a better time in towns, and they bear a grudge against the outsiders on this account and also because the outsiders are generally not much good at the work they are sent to do. Relations may be further strained when village youths try to make friends with city girls. This is not to say that relations are always bad, but conflicts appear to be quite frequent, though they are seldom mentioned in the press. Podbegaylo[13] relates that in the Voronezh region a fight broke out between local inhabitants and students of the Technological Institute engaged in agricultural work, and S., a local man, was killed. The inquiry showed that a student had hit him on the head with a wrench, after which another student had inflicted a mortal blow with the wooden handle of a pitchfork.

Fights are also quite frequent between holiday-camp visitors and the local inhabitants, particularly when local youths importune female holidaymakers. Often, if a party of visitors is dancing in a restaurant or out of doors, a local lad may ask one of the girls to dance with him and be refused. In such a case it is likely that a group of locals will waylay the party afterwards to avenge the insult to their comrade. In a case described by Podbegaylo, the victim was a soldier. At Rostov-on-Don, F., who was drunk, entered a restaurant and went up to a table at which a soldier was sitting with his girl friend. He asked the girl to dance, but she refused. F. went into the yard, waited until the couple came out, and stabbed the soldier to death with a knife. The Rostov regional court sentenced him to death for "murder committed from hooligan motives."[14]

A brawl is sometimes provoked for the express purpose of beating or killing someone. However, most fights of this kind are spontaneous, though the provocation may appear very slight to the outsider. In the Buriat republic in Central Asia, one Nikolayev was convicted of the murder "from hooligan motives" of one Tabituyev on November 21, 1961. The circumstances were these: Four natives of the Bakhtan settlement, Toronov, Dabeyev, Tabituyev, and Balbin, and three natives of the Sagan-Khalgay settlement, Alchikhanov, Dorzheyev, and Nikolayev, met for a drinking party in the house of a shopkeeper named Yankevichius. A fight broke out, and Nikolayev accused the inhabitants of the Bakhtan settlement of "seeking an easy life." Toronov and Dabeyev stopped the fight and persuaded everyone to leave. Nikolayev, Dorzheyev, Tabituyev, Balbin, and Dabeyev went to the club to see a film. Afterwards Nikolayev went up to Balbin and grabbed him by the front of his clothes. Dabeyev and Osipov parted them. On the way home Nikolayev said, "I'll shoot the lot!" He got a gun and three buckshot cartridges from his house and went back to where Osipov, Tabituyev, and the others were standing. Seeing him approaching with a gun, Dorzheyev went up to him and tried to take it away. Nikolayev fired twice; one shot hit the ground near Osipov's feet, the other wounded Tabituyev, who was taken to the hospital and died there.[15]

On this occasion the insult was perhaps not altogether trifling, but in many cases it is very slight indeed. At Barnaul,[16] a drunken man killed a stranger for refusing to buy and drink a bottle of vodka with him. Another killed his comrade for refusing to leave the club with him, and then sat and played an accordion until the police arrived.[17] M., who lived in a hostel, killed a man for breaking his plate; he was convicted of murdering from hooligan motives, and the

Supreme Court rejected the plea put forward on appeal that he had been actuated by personal revenge.[18]

Many similar cases of murder following a quarrel have been attributed to hooligan motives. Although some jurists argue that the lack of a clear motive for the crime is not a ground for presuming hooliganism, I have the impression that the courts like to find hooligan motives (an aggravating circumstance) in murders where there is no substantial motive of a traditional kind, e.g., when the act is provoked by a trifling insult or when a man starts shooting for no apparent reason. The Soviet jurist Borodin[19] has said that he knows of no case in which the murderer himself stated that he killed from hooligan motives.

Soviet law considers it an aggravating circumstance when a murder is connected with the victim's official or public activity. This applies especially to the murder of one's superior for reasons connected with work, after a reprimand for being drunk on the job, for example,[20] or if the worker is dissatisfied with his pay, like G., who believed that the foreman of his team of plasterers at the factory had calculated his wage unfairly. He piled oil-soaked cloths around the foreman's house at night and set fire to them, knowing that the foreman and his family were at home. The foreman was severely burned and died soon afterward.[21]

Drunkenness faced with official strictness often gives rise to murder: one of a group of drunken travelers murdered a female guard for refusing to let them board a train.[22]

Murders of foresters and fishery and game inspectors are quite common. Poachers accept the fact that inspectors have to earn their pay by assessing small fines from time to time, but they do not like them to show excessive zeal, and they expect them to be open to bribery if a poacher is caught in a serious offense. I know personally of cases in which inspectors who were especially conscientious and refused to be bribed were threatened with violence.

According to Soviet principles, it is the social duty of

every citizen to aid the fight against crime. This being so, the courts should include in the category of "murder connected with the victim's public activity" cases in which a man is killed trying to subdue a hooligan. Sometimes the courts do so decide, but in other cases such a murder is deemed to have been committed from hooligan motives. In a factory hostel at Rostov, a member of a Communist labor brigade reproved a man for hooligan behavior; the latter invited him to "come outside and talk about it," and killed him as soon as they were on the street.[23]

The traditional motives for murder—concealment of a crime and vengeance against a witness who has provided damaging evidence or against an informer—also operate in the Soviet Union. In the Gorky region three men murdered M. and two of her children after she reported to the police that one of them had raped her daughter.[24]

Murders committed during a theft or holdup are not, I think, frequent in the Soviet Union. Apparently only the most desperate criminals risk their skins this way. The majority, even of hardened thieves, are deterred by the severity of the penalty and the risk of being caught. Murder committed for the purpose of facilitating another crime is punishable by death, whereas the death penalty applies to stealing only if socialist property is taken on a very large scale; and the authorities appear to devote much more energy to investigating murders than crimes against property. They no doubt recognize that a man who has committed murder in the course of another crime, and has not been caught, is a special danger to society; he is already liable to the death penalty and, having nothing to lose, is quite likely to commit further murders, if only to escape detection.

One only rarely hears of cases in which individuals or groups have committed a series of deliberate murders and not been caught. Between 1949 and 1958, R.[25] committed eight murders in the RSFSR and the Ukraine, attempted three more as well as a number of holdups, and finally killed two of the policemen who were arresting him. Such cases are infrequently reported, but the authorities take them very seriously: a countrywide search is organized, and the murderer is unlikely to escape. Not long ago *Izvestia* reported the capture of one Alekseyev, who had committed several murders.[26] His photograph had been sent to police forces all over the country, and a sergeant on duty arrested him at the Sochi railroad station. Alekseyev must have been regarded as a particularly dangerous man, for the sergeant was personally congratulated by a minister and promoted to the rank of lieutenant.

A man named Ionesyan became well known to the Moscow public in the early 1960s for systematically murdering children in apartments: his crimes appeared to be the acts of a maniac, and the general belief was that his motives were sexual. The police posted photographs of him, and he was caught. Since then the police have on a few other occasions invited the public to help catch criminals, either by showing their pictures on television or by posting photographs and descriptions outside police stations, though there are far fewer of these than are seen in American post offices. Appeals of this sort are not published in the newspapers, however. In 1974 the police informed the population of Moscow about a man who had murdered seven or eight women; the Soviet press did not report the matter, although the *New York Times* did.[27]

The Soviet press apparently does not publish reports about mass murderers for fear of discrediting the police in the eyes of the public, who may not understand that it is not easy to catch a desperate criminal with nothing to lose. However, such murderers are fairly common. In the 1920s one Petrov-Komarov committed twenty-nine similar murders: he would accost a peasant at a fair, ostensibly to buy a horse from him, and invite him home to seal the bargain,

after which he plied him with drink, killed, and robbed
him.[28] In 1925, a group of brigands raided a forest area
and one of them, Fomichev, hid in a shed and murdered
nineteen men who were sent there by his accomplices. After
that, he rounded on a calf that was in the shed and with the
words, "What are you looking at?" swung his ax, killed it,
and threw it on the heap of victims.[29]

Another aggravating circumstance in Soviet law is the
definition of murder "with special cruelty." The Criminal
Code of 1926 referred only to the infliction of special pain,
but present-day jurists often extend the definition to cover
such actions as mocking or dishonoring the victim's corpse.
Borodin classes the disfiguring or burning of the body as
"special cruelty," but points out that acts of this kind do not
count as aggravating circumstances if they are committed
after the victim is dead: the law is concerned with the circumstances of the murder itself, not with indignities performed afterwards. He goes on to say that the dismemberment of the corpse is generally not proof of cruelty, since it
is usually done in order to conceal the crime. In some cases
the courts have so ruled, but this does not appear to be the
dominant view. In any case, if dismemberment is not intended to conceal the crime, it counts as special cruelty.[30]
Podbegaylo reports that two women at Kislovodsk lived in
unnatural sexual relations* with L., whom they resolved to
kill in revenge for the systematic indignities he inflicted on
them. They gave him a sleeping pill, after which one of
them struck him with an iron and killed him. They then cut
his body into thirteen pieces with a razor and, in the author's phrase, "mocked" the remains. The Stavropol regional court defined their act as murder committed with
special cruelty.[31]

---

* It is not clear what this phrase means in the context; but the moral
sensitivity of Soviet jurists is such that it may simply indicate that both
women were L.'s mistresses.

M. Lyubarsky's popular book on detection, *How Secrets Are Discovered* (Leningrad, 1968), describes the case of an elderly woman in Leningrad who committed a murder for gain, chopped up the body, and either buried the pieces or threw them into the Neva River. Her reaction to the death sentence was remarkable:

> The judge read the sentence, and the public applauded. Marfa curled her bloodless lips in a sneer and shouted at them: "Croak away, you vultures—you can smell carrion, can you?"*
>
> Then, asked whether she understood the sentence, she answered loudly, "I should think I do. A bullet in the head—any fool can understand that!"

It also counts as special cruelty if the feelings of bystanders are outraged, as, for example, if parents or children are murdered in each other's presence;[32] or, of course, if special pain is inflicted. The court does not always state its opinion on this point but the following cases have been regarded as especially cruel. In the Saratov region, I. filled the victim's respiratory tract with mud. In the Rostov region, P. poured benzine over his wife and the child in her arms and set fire to them (P. was executed by shooting). In Moscow in 1956, K., with the help of a friend, poisoned her husband by first getting him to drink vodka, then giving him sulfuric acid and caustic soda and injecting vinegar essence into his mouth with a syringe; the victim died in agony next day.[33]

Sometimes a murder committed with great cruelty has not been so defined by the court, which has found a mitigat-

---

* This is the only case I know of in which a convicted person has reacted to the applause of the audience in court. I do not know the origin of the national custom, as it may now be called, of applauding a severe sentence for a serious crime, but I imagine that it dates from Soviet times.

ing circumstance, as in the following case where "extreme mental stress" was allowed: In the Rostov region, B., while drunk, stole a bottle of Lysol from a store and invited passers-by to drink from it. Two of them did so and received internal burns. A., horrified at this, took B. to one side, knocked him down and made him drink the rest of the Lysol, which killed him.[34]

A typical form of murder committed with special cruelty is inflicting torture or multiple wounds and blows. As I have already mentioned, murder by multiple knife wounds is the traditional punishment for treachery in the criminal underworld; but the courts do not always recognize murders of this type for what they are, or perceive the quarrels that lie behind them.

In the great majority of Russian murders the methods are fairly primitive. According to A. A. Gertsenzon's 1970 study, *Criminal Law and Sociology*, 18 percent of the murders studied by him were committed by beating with the fists, kicking, or using some handy object such as a stick or stone, a log or an iron, while in 23 percent of the cases the weapon was cold steel, usually a knife. The same source claims that only 4 percent of the murders committed in Moscow are committed with firearms, while in the provinces where more people own hunting rifles, the proportion is greater; the figure for the Soviet Union as a whole is 21 percent.[35]

The lack of sophistication of most Soviet murders can be put down to the fact that the majority of those convicted have had only seven years' schooling.[36]* Of course, it may be that the use of more up-to-date murder methods and

---

* *Problems of Crime*, No. 1 (1965), notes that this goes to confirm that a basic objective of preventive work should be to raise the educational level of society. I would observe, however, that murderers do not lag far behind the rest of society in the number of years of schooling.

weapons will become possible in the USSR, but at present the most frequently used firearms are sporting rifles and sawed-off shotguns,* and the government has made a determined effort to limit their use. The sale of hunting guns is very strictly controlled;† revolvers are not sold at all, and only certain categories of State officials are allowed to possess and use them. A special article of the Criminal Code lays down penalties for manufacturing, possessing, wearing, or selling firearms (except smooth-barrel hunting rifles), ammunition, or explosives without permission. It also forbids the manufacturing, wearing, or sale of daggers, bowie knives, or similar weapons without permission, except in localities where they are part of the national costume or are reserved for official use. Special penalties attach to stealing firearms, ammunition, or explosives.

There are also special kinds of homicide like cannibalism. Cannibalism as such is not against Soviet law, and cases have been reported in connection with severe famines in various localities. In 1922 the periodical *Pravo i Zhizn* (Law and Life) published the text of two official reports on the arrest of persons charged with murder for the purpose of cannibalism. One of these (couched in garbled and illiterate language) ran as follows:

> I, People's Prosecutor of the Second District, having considered the accusation by Citizeness Yanikulova

---

* The Supreme Court has ruled that a sawed-off shotgun is to be classified as a pistol for the purpose of regulations governing the conditions in which it may be kept, manufactured, or carried on the person.

† A decree of the Council of Ministers of the USSR, No. 478, of May 11, 1959, lays down that rifles may only be sold to members of sporting clubs who can pass an elementary test in their use. In 1963 the Presidium of the RSFSR Supreme Soviet adopted decrees embodying "stronger measures against violations of the regulations governing the possession and use of firearms" and "stricter penalties for violation of hunting regulations."

of Ilyakulvin Village that Samigulla and Khatir Ziazet-dinov killed a man and used his flesh as food, and taking into account that the investigation is not yet complete and that the accused, if they remain at liberty, may evade investigation and repeat their crime elsewhere, do order on this 4th day of March 1922 . . . that Samigulla, aged forty-two, and Satir [*sic*] aged fifty-seven, be confined in the Belebeyevsky forced-labor institution of the second category. Signed: Vak-eyev. Copy certified by the clerk of the Prosecutor's office.

At about the same time, when famine was raging in the Volga District, gangs of youths engaged in cannibalism.[37] In 1946–47, according to Nikita Khrushchev (*Khrushchev Remembers: The Last Testament* [1974]), cases of cannibalism were reported in the Ukraine during a famine due to drought and a bad harvest.

Cannibalism may also be the result of superstition. Although I do not have up-to-date information, it seems likely that the ancient practices of cannibalism and necrophagy, which were recorded at the turn of the century have not completely died out. I have already mentioned the thieves' superstition about eating the heart of a newborn baby. There are similar superstitions about the supernatural properties of various parts of the body and their use in sorcery, healing the sick, and casting out the evil eye.

Levenstim's 1897 article "Superstition and Criminal Law" gives many examples and quotes an old ballad in illustration:

> I will make a bed of his arms and legs,
> a pitcher of his skull.
> I will make bowls of his eye sockets,
> beer of his blood,
> and a tallow candle from the fat of his body.

Remnants of these beliefs are probably still alive, especially in areas remote from industrial centers, but there is no information as to how far they still influence the commission of murders for magic purposes. Even if they do, it is very unlikely that the Soviet press would report the fact.

Criminals have one practical custom of a cannibalistic kind. When planning to escape from a camp, they generally try to induce a prisoner who does not belong to the underworld to go with them so that they can make a meal of him if necessity compels. A prisoner may cut off bits of his own body and eat them, or drink blood from a cellmate's opened veins. Stories of such incidents should, however, be treated with caution, as a single instance becomes a legend, and the telling of it is repeated again and again in different forms, giving the impression that it has happened many times. Nonetheless, such reliable informants as Anatoly Marchenko (*My Testimony*)[38] and Edward Kuznetsov (*Prison Diaries*) report cases of prisoners eating human flesh and drinking human blood. I have written elsewhere (*To Defend These Rights*, 1975) of the Soviet method of educating prisoners by means of hunger,[39] and it may be supposed that cannibalism in prison is due to near-starvation rather than a simple desire to vary the official menu.

There is also a good deal of evidence that human beings were murdered as sacrifices in Russia as late as the second half of the last century. These sacrifices were sporadic and not part of an accepted rite. Only an exceptional disaster, like a severe epidemic or many years of drought, recalled to popular memory this ancient method of averting the divine visitation.

In the Movogrudek district in 1885, during a severe outbreak of cholera, peasants led by a paramedic named Kozakevich lured an old woman, Lutsia Mankova, to the cemetery, pushed her into a grave they had dug and buried her alive. The Minsk Criminal Court sentenced Kozakevich to flogging and twelve years' hard labor.[40] There are reports of attempts to carry out similar sacrifices in the same region during the epidemics of 1831 and 1871. Yakushin mentions a case in 1861 in the Turukhan region, near Krasnoyarsk, in which a peasant buried alive a small girl, a relative of his, hoping this would save him and his family from an epidemic then raging.[41]

A less drastic but analogous custom was associated with the ceremony called plowing round (*opakhivanie*). At times of cattle plague, village women went round the fields in solemn procession and generally sacrificed an animal. If a man crossed their path, they regarded him as the plague and beat him unmercifully. Any man who saw the procession coming would hide or run away.[42]

To judge from publications of the late nineteenth century, Russian readers were used to hearing of human sacrifices carried out in various parts of the country to avert some calamity or other, and prosecutions for this offense were not a matter of surprise as they would be today. This helps to explain the public reaction to two notorious cases of alleged human sacrifice, the Beilis affair,[43] one of the most famous manifestations of anti-Semitism in Czarist Russia in which Mendel Beilis, a Kiev Jew, was accused in 1911 of the ritual murder of a Christian child and eventually grudgingly acquitted in 1913, and that of the Multan Votyaks, which will be described later.

There is no doubt that anti-Semitism in administrative circles played a large part in the Beilis prosecution, but this was probably not so obvious to the public then as it is now, since reports of human sacrifice were familiar to the average Russian, who on the other hand knew nothing of the Jewish religion and culture. Thus it is all the more to the credit of the Russian liberal intelligentsia that, thanks to their efforts, justice finally triumphed in the Beilis case.*

As to the Multan Votyaks,† while the judicial aspect is clear enough, the official investigation was so inept it is impossible to judge the facts impartially.

In 1895 a human body, with the head cut off and the "pectoral organs" removed, was found near the village of Stary Multan in Vyatka province, and a group of Votyak villagers were brought to trial for practicing human sacrifice. The preliminary investigation was carried out by irregular methods; the district police officer induced the peasants to confess by making them take an oath in front of

---

* Vipper, the prosecutor at Beilis' trial, was himself tried after the Revolution for his part in the affair. The prosecutor was Nikolai Krylenko, later Commissar of Justice, whose speech was printed in a volume of his public statements published in 1924.

Krylenko stated that Vipper had served after the Revolution in the Food Committee of the Kaluga province; he had been a good official and his superiors were prepared to stand bail for him. Nonetheless, Krylenko went on, "We must recognize that from the point of view of the defense of the Revolution, Citizen Vipper cannot be allowed to remain at liberty. He must be isolated, and if I am asked what I mean by 'isolated,' I reply: destroyed."

Vipper stated at his trial that during the Beilis affair he had really believed in ritual murders. He added: "I may be to blame for having somewhat extended the scope of the trial beyond the limits of the indictment. That was due to excess of zeal, and perhaps I made a mistake. I was wrong to let myself be carried away, and to press for a conviction as I did."

The editors of Krylenko's speeches add the following information: "Taking into account that, after the Revolution, Vipper had not shown active hostility to the Soviet system, but also that he was still actuated by ignorant prejudice and was therefore harmful to the Revolution, the Revolutionary Tribunal sentenced him to be confined in a concentration camp until the complete consolidation of the Communist system in the Republic." I do not know what became of him, but if he is alive I am sure he is still in custody, awaiting the "complete consolidation of the Communist system."[44]

† The Votyaks, nowadays called Udmurts, are a Finno-Ugrian tribe living on the middle Volga. They were converted to Christianity in the eighteenth century.

a stuffed bear, this being an animal much venerated by their tribe.*

Two villagers were convicted by the local court, but both sentences were quashed by the Appeals Division of the Senate, on the ground that due process had been seriously violated. The Senate's decision ordering a retrial was pronounced by the well-known lawyer A. F. Koni, who underlined its importance in the following words:

> A conviction in this case must be arrived at in strict accordance with the due forms and process of law, since by it the court authoritatively confirms the existence of a savage and frightful practice, and inevitably raises the question whether sufficient and appropriate measures have been taken, during the centuries of Russian rule over the Votyak region, to fulfill our country's mission of Christianity, civilization, and enlightenment.[46]

The retrial in fact ended in acquittal. Public attention was drawn to the case in a series of articles by the popular writer and publicist Vladimir Korolenko.[47] Like much Russian journalism on legal topics, these articles are somewhat emotional; a more dispassionate account is contained in an article in the *Bulletin of the Ministry of Justice*, (1896), No. 8.

Human sacrifice prompted by the teaching of various fanatical sects is a large subject I will not discuss in detail here. A good deal of space is devoted to it in pre-Revolutionary literature, for example in Levenstim's *Fanaticism and Crime* (1898) and in an article by Yakoby, "Criminal Punishment and Adherence to Primitive Sects" (1912). Soviet publications speak of similar practices, but these references should be treated with caution; they are fragmentary and undocumented, and the sects in question are

---

* The bear oath was also practiced by kindred peoples such as the Ostyaks.[45]

actively persecuted by the present atheistic regime. The Soviet lawyer S. V. Borodin[48] in his 1964 book on court decisions in murder cases quotes for the most part popular antireligious publications and only in one instance refers to a case recorded in the archives of the Supreme Court of the RSFSR (to which the ordinary reader has no access). This concerns the conviction, in Kalinin province, of a sixty-year-old woman of the Pentecostalist sect for murdering her year-old grandson and attempting to murder another grandson aged five; she claimed, according to Borodin, to have "heard a voice from God commanding her to sacrifice them."

Fanatical sects have certainly existed in Russia for centuries, and the Soviet persecution of religion may have increased their tendency to fanaticism as a spiritual defense against no less fanatical atheism. It is therefore interesting to study whatever reliable evidence one can find of the conflicts between the practical teachings of these sects and Soviet criminal law. Unfortunately such evidence is hard to come by, and one has to allow for prejudice in the treatment of it by Soviet jurists. Borodin, for instance, after speaking of sectarian fanaticism, adds: "It must be emphasized that savage fanaticism is to some degree inherent in every religion without exception." Reading these words one may recall the case of Bidiya Dandaron, head of a Buddhist community in the Buryat republic, who recently died in a Soviet labor camp; the "experts" at his trial duly certified that savage fanaticism was a mark of Buddhism.[49]

Murders of wizards and witches are another special type of homicide. Fear of witchcraft seems to be much less prevalent today than it was in the last century, but it has not died out, and murder for this reason is still a possibility.

The book, *Soviet Criminology* (Moscow, 1966),[50] reported a case in which a man had tried to kill a "witch" for casting a spell on him. Borodin[51] quotes at some length a case in which A. killed the "wizard" S. for causing death and disease by enchantment. More than twenty witnesses gave evidence, not about the actual murder but about A.'s record—he had previously been convicted of robbery and accused of rape; they also agreed that S. was a wizard. The witness G. said that S. had brought a disease on him which made him trip over stumps and tummocks. (Although the district court ignored the fact, this witness was a government purveyor and a habitual drunkard.) The witness M. said that S. had caused his face to swell up and had then cured it by means of a stone covered with spittle. The court solemnly recorded these depositions and much more irrelevant nonsense of the same kind. Far from condemning the witnesses' delusions, the effect of the questioning was such that the court and the public were confirmed in the belief that S. had magic powers. As Borodin observed, no reliable view of S.'s character emerged, and no light was shed on the reasons for the murder. The Supreme Court pointed out to the district court that it was its business to establish the motive for the crime and also to disabuse members of the public of their false ideas concerning S.

There are also blood feuds leading to murder. For centuries the vendetta, obliging all members of the family of a murdered man to take revenge on the murderer and his family, has prevailed among certain Asiatic peoples of the USSR, especially in the northern Caucasus.

Today revenge of this type is considered an aggravating circumstance in murder cases, and the sentence may be death. Vendetta killings appear to be much less common than they were in the nineteen twenties and thirties, and apparently the courts now take more trouble to ascertain whether or not a murder is the result of a blood feud. In a recent case,[52] the Presidium of the Supreme Court laid down that the existence of a feud should not be assumed without proof:

> In the absence of proof of a blood feud, and in view of evidence that Aushev and Toldiev were on unfriendly terms, it must be concluded that the murder was due to personal enmity.

The ambiguity here is typical of many Supreme Court rulings and decisions: it is unclear whether the deciding factor is the lack of proof of a blood feud or the evidence of personal hostility. One gets the impression that the Supreme Court wanted to leave a loophole for lower courts that would enable them, if they chose, to ignore the principle that there must be proof of a blood feud. In earlier decades, when the campaign against survivals of tribal customs was still going on, the courts were inclined to assume that any local murder among populations that observed this custom was due to a blood feud, particularly if the two families were known to be at odds. It is a good thing if this assumption no longer holds.

The history of many peoples shows that usually, over a period of time, the vendetta is gradually replaced by a system of monetary compensation or blood money. The Soviet authorities prevented this natural evolution from taking place by making it a criminal offense to give or receive such compensation. At the same time, they set up procedures for the reconciliation of feuding families.* Those who refused to be reconciled were deported. According to the *Commentary on the Criminal Code* (1971), refusal might be expressed by failing to attend a public session at the invitation of the reconciliation commission without giving an adequate excuse.

The question of responsibility in mercy killings and suicide pacts is a complex one, and I do not know that it has been satisfactorily resolved anywhere. How far it is a prob-

---

* Decree of the All-Union Central Executive Committee and the Council of People's Commissars, 1928.[53]

lem in the Soviet Union can hardly be judged by the few references to such killings in the legal journals.

One Soviet author, L. D. Gaukhman, stated in 1959 that few people are killed at their own request.[54] A rider to Article 143 of the 1922 Criminal Code provided that "a murder committed out of compassion and at the insistence of the victim is not subject to penalty." However, this rider was soon deleted, as experience showed that it facilitated "the evasion of responsibility for socially dangerous acts."[55] In a case published in the 1920s, Zakharov, a member of the Communist Party, showed the deputy public prosecutor of Saratov province a certificate signed by another Party member, Bolshakov, and two witnesses, to the effect that Bolshakov no longer wished to live and desired Zakharov to shoot him. Zakharov did so and relied for his defense on the article quoted above.

At the present time mercy killing is usually treated as deliberate homicide without aggravating circumstances (Article 103 of the Criminal Code). In one case of murder by request tried by the Supreme Court, the victim, who was killed in the forest by two rifle shots, was a schizophrenic who had asked to be shot; it is not clear if the murderer knew of the victim's mental illness. The Judicial Collegium of the Supreme Court observed that he had previously contemplated suicide, as shown by notes of his which were exhibited in evidence.*

Suicide pacts are a particular case of murder by request. In 1960 in the Yakut republic in northern Siberia, Puzynin, a truck driver, and Kasyanova, the wife of a Red Army soldier, became lovers, intending to divorce their respective spouses and marry each other.[56] Their relatives and workmates tried to dissuade them. Convinced that they could not live without each other, they decided to commit suicide,

---

* *Collected Decrees and Decisions of the Criminal Division of the RSFSR Supreme Court 1964–1972* (Moscow, 1974), p. 247.

and Kasyanova wrote a note to that effect. On the night of January 9/10, 1961, Puzynin took Kasyanova to his apartment and, as they had agreed, shot her in the head. He then tried to kill himself and suffered serious injuries, which necessitated a major operation. The Presidium of the Supreme Court found that he had killed Kasyanova with her consent and had tried to commit suicide, and that his crime was one of murder without aggravating circumstances.

In some instances, of course, one or the other party to a suicide pact may not be acting in good faith. The following case is reported by N. I. Zagorodnikov in *Crimes Against Life* (Moscow, 1961): K., to avoid paying alimony, persuaded M., who was carrying his child, to commit suicide with him. She hanged herself, but K. did not carry out his part of the pact and took no steps to rescue her. The Supreme Court of the USSR found him guilty of deliberate murder "from base motives" and of contriving circumstances in which to carry out his crime, which, the Court ruled, fell squarely under Article 136 of the 1926 Criminal Code—premeditated murder committed under aggravating circumstances.

Soviet doctrine, to judge from Soviet legal writings, is that "intentional incitement to suicide constitutes deliberate murder."[57] The 1971 Commentary on the Criminal Code states that persuading a minor or a person of unsound mind to commit suicide constitutes deliberate murder by exploiting the mental peculiarities of the victim.

Dueling is a very minor problem in the USSR. I know of only one instance of a man who was tried by a Soviet court for killing his opponent in a duel. This was Tertov, a pupil at the Military Academy, in 1923. The Supreme Court defined it as a murder committed for base motives, because dueling was a survival of feudal aristocratic traditions. The weekly *Soviet Justice* (1923, No. 8) reported the case:

Knowing that dueling is a feudal survival practiced exclusively by officers of the old czarist army and by the nobility and gentry as a means of protecting the honor of their caste by bloodshed, and that it is completely foreign to the spirit of proletarian society and the Red Army, Tertov, being a pupil at the Military Academy and thus training to be a leader of the Workers' and Peasants' Red Army, accepted a challenge to duel in which he killed his comrade Dyakonov. In so doing Tertov displayed a caste-ridden and feudal attitude, alien and inimical to proletarian society and to the Red Army, and dishonored his calling as a Red warrior and prospective leader of the Red Army.

Tertov was sentenced to eighteen months' imprisonment, the reason for leniency being that "this is the first instance of a duel in Soviet judicial practice." From the proceedings of the Plenum of the Supreme Court[58] it appears that a woman was involved: the Military Collegium of the Supreme Court decreed that Citizeness Mochabeli, as a socially dangerous individual, be forbidden for three years to reside in the national capital or in any major provincial town.

Killing for hire is also infrequent in the Soviet Union. In a case reported by Zagorodnikov,[59] one R. killed a woman in 1954 and received as a reward her property and the sum of 500 rubles. In another case, a woman, Z., was convicted of hiring K. to murder her husband for 300 rubles, the equivalent of two months' pay for a skilled worker.

In the Russian underworld, human lives are sometimes staked in a game of cards or dice. When a gambler has lost all he possesses and still wants to play, he may offer, if he loses again, to kill a particular individual or even the first person who turns up, if the game is being conducted in some lonely place like a cemetery. If a woman is the stake, it may be agreed that the winner shall possess her before she is killed. There are also reports of human lives being staked at card games in labor camps.

In the Asiatic regions of the USSR, especially Georgia, there have been cases in which a man lost a sister or a bride in a dice game and committed suicide rather than fulfill the bargain. These were generally young men who had been enticed into gambling but had not yet thrown off traditional feelings.

Zagorodnikov[60] reports a case tried by the Supreme Court, which involved K., a worker at a machine and tractor station, and his mistress T. One day K. informed T. that he had lost her at cards and she would have to be killed unless they found a substitute victim. T., terrified, agreed to produce someone. She and K. decided on the time and method of the murder and that the victim would be a newly hired combine operator. On the evening of June 25, 1955, T., equipped with a razor, went to the collective farm's clubhouse. At about two in the morning she met M., made friends with him and asked him to take her home. K., who, according to plan, was waiting behind some buildings, attacked and pinioned M., and they dragged him into a field, where T. slashed his face and neck. When M. fell to the ground, K. stood on his chest while T. continued to inflict cuts with the razor, from which he died.

Infanticide and child murder are fairly common in Russia. The great majority of infanticide victims (87 percent according to selective data[61]) are illegitimate babies whom their parents wish to conceal or whom they do not want the burden of maintaining. For example, R., a State farm worker, became pregnant as the result of a casual liaison while her husband was on a protracted mission in the north. Unable to get an abortion in time, she concealed her pregnancy until the last moment, afraid of facing her husband's relatives and ashamed of what her acquaintances would say. The baby was born while she was outdoors at a silo. She smothered it in a cloth, made sure it was not breathing, and buried it. Postnatal complications set in, she fell ill, and her crime was discovered.

V., who had previously been married, became pregnant. She applied for an abortion too late, and it was refused. The baby was born at a maternity home. While nursing it she poured acetic acid into its mouth. She tried to put the blame for its death on the hospital staff, but without success.[62]

The Supreme Court of the Komi autonomous republic sentenced I. to eight years' imprisonment for drowning a child in a public toilet after giving birth to it on the street. The Supreme Court of the RSFSR reduced the sentence to three years on the grounds that she was in bad health at the time, was not living with the child's father, worked as a loader, had no home of her own, and repented of her crime.

G., who lived in Taganrog, a port on the Sea of Azov, became pregnant from a casual liaison. In April 1961, her eighth month of pregnancy, she gave birth prematurely to a child which her mother, who was present, drowned in a slop pail. Her mother was found guilty of murder.[63]

Cases like these are not, of course, confined to the present day. The history of social measures connected with infanticide in Russia[64] goes back to the late seventeenth century, when the first orphanage for "children of shame" was established in the reign of Peter the Great. In 1712 Peter commanded that similar orphanages be created in provincial towns so that the mothers of unwanted babies "should not commit a more grievous sin, to wit murder." A ukase of 1715 ordained that those who wished to abandon children should be allowed to deliver them to the orphanage through a window "in such sort that the persons' faces be not seen." Later sovereigns, especially Catherine the Great, showed an interest in the care of foundlings, but in 1828, under Nicholas Í, the establishment of further homes was forbidden "to avoid corrupting public morality." The pre-Revolutionary jurist N. N. Belyavsky, who set down these facts in *Police Law* (Petrograd, 1915), observed that this led to a great increase in the number of "women practicing the frightful trade of infanticide." In 1898, the prohibition was revoked. Both infanticide and the abandonment of children became widespread after the Revolution and Civil War. A Soviet source of 1932 revealed that women's welfare services in town and country were engaged in a "planned campaign" to cope with the "problem of unmarried mothers and abandoned children."[65]

In the 1920s, the neglect of a newborn child came under the heading of "failing to give assistance," and the penalty was fairly light. Subsequently a more serious view was taken, and it is now generally classed as murder or manslaughter according to circumstances.[66] Abandoning children, even on the premises of an orphanage or nursery, was classified in the early Soviet period as "failure to give assistance to a person in danger."[67]

Today the State accepts responsibility for abandoned or unwanted children. A woman who has given birth to a child may, in principle, refuse to take it away from the maternity home, though to judge from the reported cases it appears that if she so decides, the staff appeals to her sense of shame in no uncertain terms. Occasionally the press reports cases ("unworthy of Soviet womanhood") in which a mother has disowned her child in this way. It would be to the good of society if legislators and social workers took a leaf out of Peter I's book and provided a way for women to give unwanted children into protective care without making themselves known, and thus without being liable to prosecution or ignominy. This would certainly reduce instances of infanticide and of dangerously late abortions.

The murder of older children seems to be less common than infanticide, and it is generally committed by men. The motives are various: in the Rostov region in 1961, P., while drunk, quarreled with his wife and, to spite her, pulled their five-month-old child out of the cradle by its legs and knocked its head three times against a stone, killing it instantly.[68]

I. was convicted by the Ivanov District Court in 1959 of deliberately murdering his son. Wishing to abandon his wife and children and to escape claims for alimony, he made the child, aged ten, drink tea containing caustic soda. The child died a year later of complications due to corrosion of the esophagus. The forensic report stated that the administering of a strong solution of caustic soda had undoubtedly caused grievous bodily harm. I., when found out, confessed that he had intended to murder the child.[69]

T. took a three-year-old girl to a lonely place, undressed her, held her by the legs and swung her against a brick wall. Her head was smashed, and she died instantly. T., who had not previously done the girl any harm, was actuated by sexual motives.[70]

A special case of child murder is the killing of "monsters" for reasons of compassion or superstition. Article 1469 of the pre-Revolutionary Penal Code[71] provided that "if a woman has given birth to an unnaturally deformed child or even one that lacks human shape, and if any person, instead of informing the proper authority, out of ignorance or superstition puts to death a creature which, since it is born a human being, is possessed of a soul, that person shall be deprived of all personal property rights and privileges and shall be subjected to correctional detention." There is no special provision in Soviet law on the killing of malformed infants, which presumably falls under the general heading of murder, and it is unlikely that contemporary courts would regard compassionate motives as necessarily a mitigating circumstance.

*   *   *

Before 1936, abortion was a crime in Soviet law only if carried out by unqualified persons or in nonmedical institutions. There were penalties, however, for persuading a woman to abort her child.

A decree of 1936 forbade abortion except on special medical grounds, and it became a criminal offense for a woman to terminate her pregnancy. The decree, which was much discussed in the press, also provided for aid to mothers of large families. Soviet authors treated the law as a natural consequence of the "increased material welfare" of working women, which, as a writer in *Soviet Justice* (1936), No. 18, pointed out, eliminated the necessity for abortions. The same journal reported that the discussion of the law prior to its enactment had "literally involved every working man and woman in the country" and had filled them with "immense enthusiasm and inspiration, profound gratitude to the Party and government, and boundless love for our great Stalin."[72]

To discourage offenses against the new law it was necessary to improve the care of pregnant women. A writer in *Soviet Legality* (1936), No. 11, observed: "Once a woman is pregnant, social organizations such as trade unions, the government health service, and labor protection authorities owe her the utmost attention, care and even respect."[73]

The prohibition naturally increased the number of unsanitary back-street abortions and of women suffering from dangerous complications as a result. A woman in this situation often went to her doctor, and he—obliged by the authorities, in this as in other ways, to perform police functions—would report that she had had an abortion. The woman would be pressed to reveal the abortionist's name, and in some cases was refused treatment unless she did so.*

---

* There is evidence that the same technique is used nowadays to oblige sufferers from venereal disease to give the names of those with whom they have had intercourse.

Nonetheless, clandestine abortions continued to flourish, though many women were deterred by the risk involved.

In 1954 it was made legal for a woman to have her pregnancy terminated in a State hospital for a low fee. Soviet jurists observed that this brought a sharp decrease in the number of private abortions, in mortality from abortion, and in infanticide. There was, however, one factor that deterred women from using the State facilities: it was the practice to keep them in the hospital for some time after the operation, and they therefore needed a certificate of disability to explain their absence from work. This certificate included a diagnosis column, and, rather than advertise their private life in this way, many women still preferred to have abortions in secret. According to information from the Kursk region in 1961,[74] about a quarter of all women who had resorted to private abortionists and were subsequently questioned said that they had done so to prevent others from knowing that they were pregnant.

The problem of reconciling medical secrecy with the need to certify the cause of hospitalization has been discussed in Soviet legal literature. One article suggested that in abortion the diagnosis should be given as social trauma: the author chose this because, in general, medical benefits are not paid for either social trauma or abortion. However, pregnancy can seldom be called the result of a social trauma, so that the proposal really amounts to making a false declaration. Moreover it would probably not help much, as social trauma is a fairly rare diagnosis and the reader of the certificate would doubtless know what to conclude. So far as I can remember, no one has suggested doing away with the diagnosis column altogether.

A Soviet jurist writes that "suicide is profoundly contrary to Communist morality and is a manifestation of cowardice inadmissible in a member of our society. Nevertheless, Soviet legislation has never treated it as a criminal offense."[75] This is a true statement as to the law, but there is evidence that in Stalin's day prisoners who tried to commit suicide were punished for attempted sabotage.

At present, unsuccessful suicides are generally committed to psychiatric hospitals; depending on the doctor's opinion, they may not be kept there very long.* The International Covenant on Civil and Political Rights, which was ratified by the USSR and went into force in 1976, contains a provision safeguarding the right to life; this may be taken to include the right to dispose of one's own life, and therefore to commit suicide. I do not suppose, however, that all legal authorities would accept this reasoning, let alone all Soviet ones.

It is an offense under Article 107 of the Criminal Code to "induce a person materially or otherwise dependent on the guilty party to commit suicide or attempt to do so, by treating him cruelly or systematically injuring his personal dignity."† This crime is punishable by deprivation of freedom for up to five years. The evidence suggests that this crime is generally committed as a result of family disputes or, less often, quarrels at work.

There is evidence that Soviet courts construe the phrase "otherwise dependent" pretty widely. For instance, when two members of the Pentecostalist sect of Shakers committed suicide, the Moscow District Court sentenced the lead-

---

* Under an order of 1971,[76] hospitalization in such cases is a matter of administrative decision, requiring no endorsement by the courts or the public prosecutor.

† Note the curious use of the expression "the guilty party." According to Article 13 of the Code of Criminal Procedure, "No one shall be deemed guilty of a crime or subjected to penal sanctions except by a court sentence." Anomalies of this kind are frequent in Soviet legislative texts. A verdict phrased logically under Article 107 would have to say that "X is found guilty inasmuch as, being a guilty party, he induced Y to commit suicide."

ers and preachers of the sect under Article 107, stating that the accused, "being leaders and preachers of the prohibited religious sect of Pentecostalist Shakers, systematically conducted assemblies and prayer meetings of the sectarians, accompanied by superstitious rites producing a state of exaltation. They inculcated into members of the sect the belief that any sacrifices should be accepted for the sake of eternal life. By these superstitions and suggestions they brought to a state of derangement, and finally to suicide, the working woman N. and also K., a mother of three children, who, before making away with herself, twice tried to kill her small daughter."[77]

Suicide statistics are not published in the Soviet Union at the present time so it is hard to say which age groups and sections of the population are most affected. A Soviet author[78] states that suicides by juveniles do occur but are very rare, "which is understandable, as there is no social basis for such conflicts."

Article 105 of the Criminal Code provides that homicide committed while exceeding the limits of necessary self-defense is punished by deprivation of freedom for up to two years or by correctional labor (without deprivation of freedom) for up to one year.

The question of the limits within which force can properly be used to repel an unlawful attack on oneself or on others is a complex one and has been variously answered by Soviet legal authorities. Here I am mainly concerned with how far Russian public opinion coincides with Soviet juridical practice.

In the nineteenth century, there was some difference between the attitude of the legislators and courts on the one hand and public opinion on the other. In particular, the public was inclined to approve acts that went beyond necessary self-defense, even, for instance, "the murder of an aggressor after the assault was over or when the danger had passed."[79] Similar sentiments seem to prevail at the present time. According to a Soviet report in 1961–67, cases of "delayed self-defense" accounted for more than a quarter of all convictions for exceeding the limits of necessary self-defense, which suggests that there is some confusion in the popular mind between self-defense and revenge.

It would appear that in some ways public opinion today is more indulgent in this respect than it was formerly. Alexander Solzhenitsyn, who often accurately reflects the legal consciousness of the Russian public, speaks of the law on self-defense as "most absurd."*

There are several indications that popular feeling does not sanction murder in defense of property. This accords with Soviet juridical practice: owners of gardens or orchards who shoot at marauders have been convicted of murder or grievous bodily harm. It is not clear, however, whether this applies to the defense of "socialist (i.e., public) property."

Soviet jurists have debated whether the victim of an attack is entitled to plead self-defense if circumstances made it possible for him to have run away. Present practice inclines to answer this in the affirmative. In one case the

---

* In *The Gulag Archipelago*, Vol. 2, Solzhenitsyn indignantly quotes the case of Alexander Zakharov, a Red Army soldier, who was attacked by a hooligan outside a clubhouse. He took out his pocketknife and killed the hooligan for which he was sentenced to ten years for second-degree murder.

The fact that Zakharov was a Red Army man is significant. Popular judgment is apt to discriminate between persons and often pays more attention to the background of those involved than to the circumstances of the case. This is particularly true when there is a difference of backgrounds. The story would be very differently judged if it went: "A hooligan was attacked by a Red Army soldier." It is the contrast rather than the individual background that counts: people may be aware that Red Army soldiers often despoiled the populations of conquered territories, but this does not prevent them from reacting instinctively in favor of a Red Army man over a hooligan.[80]

Plenum of the Supreme Court of the USSR ruled that the Supreme Court of the RSFSR had illegally reversed the acquittal of D., who was attacked by some drunken hooligans, ran away from them and, to escape further pursuit, threw a stone which gravely injured one of the aggressors. The Supreme Court of the RSFSR quashed the acquittal on the ground that D. had no need to throw the stone: he was near enough to a hostel, where others could have come to his aid.[81] The USSR Supreme Court decision reaffirmed the acquittal, indicating that present legal thinking accords with popular prejudice and considers defense against attack justified even when flight is possible.

7
Sexual Crimes

Rape is the most frequent sexual crime in Russia, and the circumstances surrounding it are probably much the same as elsewhere, although it is hard to be certain, since the Soviet press and legal publications are careful not to risk corrupting the reader with too much information about this fairly widespread crime.*

It should be noted that sexual freedom is more limited in Russia than in the West, not as a matter of law but because of social tradition and the tendency to mind other people's business. As far as the law is concerned, Western codes with their relics of Puritanism tend to be more restrictive than the Soviet. Soviet law does not take cognizance of adultery or extramarital relations; abortion is legal, and divorce procedure simple. But traditions that impose sexual restraints are quite strong, especially in the provinces, and many factors of Soviet life tend to reinforce them—not least the community's interference in the affairs of the individual, which plays such an important part in Soviet ideology. Extramarital relations, for instance, are an object of curiosity

* According to Gertsenzon,[1] convictions for rape amounted to 1.7 percent of all convictions in the USSR in 1966.

and disapproval on the part of organized groups, and extra-marital pregnancy is often condemned at public meetings. Trade union, Komsomol (Communist Youth League), and Party organizations consider it their duty to look after the moral standards of their members and think nothing of publicly exposing delinquencies, often to a delighted audi-ence. (The average citizen tries to duck Party meetings as far as possible, but he makes an exception when the agenda includes the item "personal matters.") *

These standards do not affect men to the same degree as women; the sexual freedom of Soviet women is consider-ably hampered by the outspokenness of public criticism and by the fact that, outside of the largest cities, practically no acceptable methods of contraception are available.

It would be naïve to attribute the frequency of rape in the Soviet Union exclusively to the effect of strait-laced atti-tudes, but it can safely be said that in many cases it is due to sexual deprivation rather than to perversion. There are, of course, men who find sexual satisfaction in violence as such, but I believe they are a comparatively small propor-tion of those who commit rape, although sexual hunger may, of course, also contain elements of sadism.

The types of situations in which rape occurs are largely what might be expected. A frequent instance is that of a girl or woman without a protector who becomes involved in drunken revelry. According to data published in *Questions in the Struggle Against Crime* (1965), No. 17, 55 percent of the victims were drunk when raped, and 30 percent had

* It has been observed that people in the USSR say one thing at meetings and another in private; I have frequently heard them express indignation at the public ventilation of the intimate affairs of others. Popular stories that make the rounds also suggest that group interfer-ence in private affairs is unpopular. One of these describes the embarrass-ment of the organizers of a public inquisition when a Komsomol member, asked who was responsible for her pregnancy, immediately named three other members of the organization. Nevertheless the inquisitions go on and are often used as a means of settling private scores.

previously been drinking with the men concerned. A later report in the same journal (1972), No. 15, stated that over 50 percent of the occurrences of rape took place "under the influence of drink" in circumstances that did not in themselves suggest that any crime was intended. In many cases the woman behaves provocatively and her companion, taking consent for granted, becomes excited to such a degree that he cannot control himself when she later resists. The courts tend to regard the victim's provocative conduct or bad reputation as a mitigating circumstance.

In the case of one Permyakov[2] the court found that his victim, A., "had previously behaved indecorously, drunk to excess, and formed liaisons with chance acquaintances. Permyakov was aware of this from a friend of hers and was thus encouraged to behave as he did. When A. resisted, he threatened to give her a beating she would 'remember all her life,' and in fact hit her several times." Taking into account A.'s conduct and the sincere repentance of the accused, the court sentenced him to five years' imprisonment.*

* The fact that the courts take into account a woman's previous liaisons may be connected with the Russian moral tradition. In Russia, as in many Asiatic countries, virginity is considered a moral value as well as a recommendation from the sexual point of view. An article published in 1965 (Minskaya, *Questions in the Struggle Against Crime*, No. 17) remarks that "virginity is a kind of certificate of moral purity."

Popular opinion seems to regard it as more reprehensible to rape a virgin. If an unmarried woman is known not to be a virgin, public opinion is less offended by a sexual attack on her, though it may still censure the use of undue violence. In a case reported in the 1920s,[3] one of the accused gave evidence as follows:

> I went back with K. to the bathhouse where the woman N. was, and people were talking about whether she was a respectable woman (i.e., a virgin). *On this occasion* [present author's italics] they sent me for a lamp and she was examined. It turned out that she wasn't respectable, and S. gave her to us and said, "Here, take her!" A witness stated that all seven of the accused then had intercourse with N., some of them twice. They maintained, however, that it was with her consent.

Sometimes a woman is deliberately made so drunk as to be unaware of what is happening. In a case some years ago,[4] a countryman named Semenenko was giving a party prior to joining the army. One of his guests, Krivunenko, made a woman drunk, took her out of doors and raped her, after which she was put to bed in the yard. He then suggested to the others that they should all take her into the garden and rape her one by one. While they did so, one of the men stood guard and prevented some boys from approaching the scene.

It quite often happens that a girl who has met a man on the street or in the company of acquaintances agrees to let him take her home or even goes to his place. The press recently reported the case of a girl who casually met a group of young men, went home with one of them and was raped by the whole lot. Before she left they told her to say nothing and made her sign a note declaring she had been recruited and paid by a foreign intelligence service; they told her that if she informed against them they would send this to the KGB. Frightened as she no doubt was, she trusted in Soviet justice and did inform the authorities.

As in other countries, a great many cases of rape are never reported because the victims do not want them known. Their attitude may be due to shame, concern for their reputations, unwillingness to be "dragged through the courts," or in many cases, fear of revenge by the rapist or his friends. Often the victim's parents inform the police on finding that the woman is pregnant; but if she is of age she must herself make an oral or written declaration before there can be a prosecution, unless there are aggravating circumstances. In some cases the rapist forces his victim to go to the authorities by boasting to his friends that he has raped her and got off scot-free, thus creating a risk that others will try to do the same.

It can also happen that a woman who has complained of rape changes her mind, either spontaneously or under pressure, and, feeling sorry for the accused, declares to the court that she did not mean to inform against him and is willing to marry him. It is exceptional in such cases for the man to be let off without punishment, and the woman runs the risk of being called to account for knowingly making a false accusation, unless it is shown that she was talked into doing so.

There are many instances of ill-intentioned women bringing false charges of rape against male neighbors, acquaintances, and even strangers. It is sometimes difficult for the courts to know whether such a woman is lying, especially as there is often an element of violence even in voluntary sexual relations, traces of which are evident to the forensic expert. Sometimes the women do not bother much about the plausibility of their stories. In one case a woman said she had been raped in a henhouse by the man she was living with; it was pointed out that there were no traces of chicken droppings on her clothes, whereupon she confessed that she wanted to spite the man because he would not marry her.[5]

A woman may also be genuinely but mistakenly convinced that an attempt has been made to rape her. In Chita[6] one Dneprovsky was accused of knocking a woman down on the street and trying to rape her. His defense was that he had been drunk and had knocked her down by accident, whereupon she started shouting "rape." The Supreme Court of the RSFSR found that the woman's story was inconsistent and dismissed the case.

A man tried for rape by the Leningrad District Court said that he had asked the woman, a neighbor of his, into his room to borrow some money from her for a drink. He shut the door and before he could say a word, she rushed to the window, broke it, and started shouting. Fearing that the neighbors would come running and would believe the worst, he grabbed her arm to pull her away from the window and put a hand over her mouth to stop her screaming. In the struggle they both fell on the floor. He said he had no intention of trying to rape the woman and had done nothing that might suggest otherwise. His wife testified that he had asked her for money for a drink that evening and that she had refused. The Collegium of the Supreme Court referred the matter back for further investigation.[7]

If there are aggravating circumstances, a prosecution for rape may be instituted independently of any complaint by the victim, e.g., in cases of collective rape or grave physical injury.*

Aggravating circumstances seem to occur frequently: in 1966, 85 percent of all cases of rape tried by the courts came under this heading.[8] It follows that most prosecutions take place independently of a complaint by the victim. According to Gertsenzon, in about one third of the cases rape is committed by a group, usually of two or three men. It is noteworthy that Soviet legal practice uses the term "collective rape" to denote either the rape of one woman by two or more men, or the case in which several men violate a group of women, though each woman is raped by only one of them.[9] In fact, the rape of one woman by two men may not be considered collective rape if they did not assist each other, as in the case of Tereshkov and Kozyukov,[10] who were tried for collective rape in the Leningrad region in 1973. Tereshkov took M., a minor who was drunk, into the

---

* The question may then arise as to whether the victim is entitled to refuse to assist the investigation or allow herself to be physically examined. As far as I know Soviet legislation does not rule on this either way.

Rape without aggravating circumstances is punishable by imprisonment ranging from three to seven years. For a second offense, or for rape accompanied by grievous bodily harm or the threat of murder, the penalty is from five to ten years. For gang rape or the rape of a minor, or if the criminal is a specially dangerous recidivist, or if the consequences are particularly serious, the punishment is death or imprisonment from eight to fifteen years, with or without subsequent exile.

forest and raped her. Kozyukov, a stranger to Tereshkov, had been watching from behind some bushes; he came up and asked Tereshkov if he too might rape the girl. Tereshkov agreed, and Kozyukov had intercourse with M. The Supreme Court ruled that this was not a case of collective rape.

In a fair number of cases the victim is murdered so as to conceal the crime. Here are three instances in which the death penalty was imposed:

K., attempting to commit rape and encountering resistance, killed his victim by hitting her repeatedly on the head with an ax. He also killed her eighty-four-year-old mother in the same way when she ran up on hearing the noise.

A man who had raped a ten-year-old girl strangled her and threw her body into a well.[11]

S. met a woman in the woods, threatened her with a knife, raped her and stole her money; she had just collected a State grant for having a large number of children. He then bound her arms, blindfolded and gagged her with a rag wrapped round a stick, slashed her belly and breast with the knife, and left her for dead. However, she was able to crawl to the highway and was rescued.

A rapist may also kill his victim in the course of overcoming her resistance. In a case of this kind a man strangled the woman he was raping and then fell into a drunken sleep, in which state he was found by the police.

Murder of the victim, either to avoid detection or to overcome resistance, may of course be prompted by sadistic motives as well. Cases of extreme sadism are apparently rare, but here are several examples. In Leningrad, G. fractured his victim's bones in thirty-five places and inflicted over a hundred bruises and abrasions.[12] In the Altai region in Central Asia, B., encountering resistance from a woman he was trying to rape, ruptured her peritoneum, dragged out nearly the whole of the small intestine, and left her bleeding in the snow; she died in a few hours.[13] Turnev, when drunk, met in the street F., a stranger to him, and tried to rape her. He hit her on the head, and she tried to run away. He hit her again, knocked her down, dragged her by the hair into some shrubbery, and raped her, having first bitten her all over the body and bitten off her nose.

If the rapist's victim is under age (under eighteen) it is a serious aggravating circumstance, and the penalty may be death. Gertsenzon states[14] that in over a third of the convictions for rape the victims were minors. The rapist may be unaware of the victim's age, but this is not always accepted as a defense.

The rape of very young girls does not seem to be common, but there is a case on record of a child of fifteen months being violated by her father.[15]* In a case in the Kherson region near the Black Sea, M., who had been drinking in a friend's house, snatched up the latter's three-year-old daughter, took her into the garden and raped her, inflicting bodily injury.[16] Another rapist met a girl of seven on a path and dragged her into the bushes. He clutched her by the throat and began to rape her, but seeing she was unconscious, took fright and ran away, thinking he had killed her.[17]

I do not know the maximum age at which women have been raped, but there are cases of very elderly victims.

In 1928 the Supreme Court ruled that a man who married a woman with the intention of divorcing her after having sexual intercourse was liable to the same penalty as for rape.[18] I have not come across any case of this kind in recent practice; the ruling seems to be an instance of the principle of analogy, already discussed. Not all jurists agreed with it at the time: the *Ukrainian Journal of Soviet Justice*[19] published an article expressing doubt that tricking

---

* According to Gertsenzon, 16 percent of all rape victims were daughters, nieces, or stepdaughters of the accused.

a woman into marriage for the purpose of intercourse could be equated with physical violence.

The penalty in the RSFSR for sexual relations with a person below the age of puberty is up to three years' imprisonment; up to six years if the act is for the purpose of "satisfying sexual passion in a perverted form."

According to Gertsenzon, this crime accounted for 0.2 percent of all convictions in 1966. Very few details of such cases are published, and it is not clear at what age criminal responsibility begins. According to the 1971 *Commentary on the RSFSR Criminal Code*,[20] "the perpetrator of this crime is, as a rule, a person who has reached his majority. Sexual intercourse between minors may involve criminal responsibility from the age of sixteen onwards in certain cases, e.g., if the age of the parties is widely different or if there are serious consequences." The *Commentary* adds that responsibility is aggravated "if sexual intercourse with a person who has not attained puberty takes place in a perverted manner, or if it is performed naturally but is accompanied by biological perversions (sadism, masochism) or social ones, e.g., collective intercourse."

To judge from the *Commentary* and from other legal literature the problem of the sexual protection of children under the age of puberty has been insufficiently studied. This may be because the assaults are few and the Soviet censorship is strait-laced, or it may be that the authorities wish to leave themselves latitude in interpreting the law on this subject.

The same is true of the law covering the corruption of minors,* except that the notion of corruption can be

---

* Depraved actions with respect to minors shall be punished by deprivation of freedom up to three years (Article 120 of the Criminal Code).

stretched even more widely. However, acts of debauchery with minors accounted for only 0.3 percent of all convictions in 1966.[21]

The *Commentary*[22] states that such acts "may take the form of *indecent* contacts, gestures, and *conversations* [present author's italics], introducing a minor to pornographic literature, pictures, or objects, performing sexual acts in front of minors, teaching minors sexual perversions, etc." *The Course of Soviet Criminal Law*[23] defines the matter in greater detail under four heads:

(1) The commission of sexual acts with the minor, as by satisfying or exciting sexual passion *per os, inter femora*, etc.; (2) persuading or compelling a minor to perform an act in relation to the guilty party, e.g., masturbation; (3) performing sexual acts in the minor's presence (exhibitionism, onanism, intercourse, etc.); (4) inducing or compelling minors to perform sexual acts together.

This account does not mention indecent conversations or pornographic literature, pictures, and objects, and the scope of the law is thus narrowed to an important extent. The authors of *The Course of Soviet Criminal Law*[24] observe that "acts of debauchery" must "have an objectively sexual character and be capable of exerting a corrupting influence on the persons affected." If judicial practice were guided by these criteria there could be some debate in particular cases as to what actions are "objectively sexual." A Soviet court would, I hope, regard it as evident that, for example, a conversation using obscene language on a nonsexual topic would not be "objectively sexual." In doing so it would be adopting a narrower interpretation of the law on corrupting minors than the authors of the *Commentary*,[25] for a conversation on any subject would certainly be regarded by a Soviet court as "indecent" if it were full of obscene language.

A man who compels a woman to have intercourse or to satisfy his sexual passion in any other way may be imprisoned for up to three years, but only if she is dependent on him materially or occupationally. Gertsenzon found this crime accounted for only 0.006 percent of all convictions in 1966. The authors of the *Commentary* state that the coercion must take the form of exploiting the woman's dependence, e.g., by finding fault with her work, depriving her of bonuses and allowances, threatening dismissal or transfer to lower-paid work, or threatening to evict her from a hostel or her home. Very few cases have been published, but there is a ruling by the Supreme Court to the effect that a superior who merely invites a woman working under him to enter into a sexual liaison is not committing a punishable offense.[26]

The penalty for homosexual acts is up to five years' imprisonment, up to eight years if committed with a minor or by exploiting the position of a dependent or if accompanied by physical force or threats.

From the Revolution until 1933 sodomy between consenting adults was not a crime in Russia proper, though it was in Azerbaijan, Georgia, and the Turkmen and Uzbek republics. It is not quite clear why the law was changed; the matter was given a political complexion, however, and in 1936 the Commissar of Justice Krylenko explained it as follows:

> It is for doctors to decide in each specific case whether the accused is a sick man or not. But if we have no reason to think he is sick, and he nonetheless commits these acts, then we say to him: "My good fellow, there's no place for you here. Among us workers, who

believe in normal relations between the sexes and who are building up a society on healthy principles, there is no room for gentry of this sort." Who in fact are our chief customers in this line? Are they working men? Of course not—they are either the dregs of society, or remnants of the exploiting classes. (*Applause.*) They don't know what to do with themselves, so they take to pederasty. (*Laughter.*) And beside them, along with them, there is another kind of work that goes on in little filthy dens and hiding places, and that is the work of counter-revolution.*

That is why we take these disorganizers of our new social system, the system we are creating for men and women and working people—we put these gentlemen on trial and we give them sentences of up to five years.

The authors of *The Course of Soviet Criminal Law*[27] rightly observe that "no attempt has been made in Soviet juridical literature to establish a clear scientific basis for making voluntary sodomy a criminal offense. The ground usually adduced, that the offender is morally corrupt and violates the laws of social morality, cannot be regarded as sufficient, for defects of personality are not a ground of criminal responsibility, and an immoral action is not necessarily a crime." The writers add that "there are serious doubts as to the expediency of continuing to treat sodomy without aggravating circumstances as a criminal offense," and they observe that the legislation of some countries, including some socialist countries, tends increasingly to make adult homosexual relations nonpunishable by law.

Details of actual prosecutions for sodomy are scarcely ever published, though the number of cases is not negligible (0.1 percent of all convictions in 1966).[28]

---

* The Soviet authorities in the 1930s apparently took seriously the alleged connection between pederasty and politics, and homosexuality was investigated by the State security apparatus. I don't know how things are today.

The need to conceal their inclinations from the outside world has led male homosexuals in Russia to form a secret subculture with its own ethical and linguistic code, analogous to those of the underworld but less sharply defined. However, this special society has been studied almost not at all, or at least nothing about it has been published.

I am not concerned here with the general causes of homosexuality, but it is a socially important fact that homosexual propensities are often acquired in prison as a result of coercion by other prisoners. The experience in many countries shows that prison authorities are unable to protect those under their care from being corrupted in this manner. In my opinion a man who has suffered in this way is entitled to demand redress from the authorities who placed him in a position where he was unable to resist the assault on his sexual integrity. I have written elsewhere of the similarity between the problems of the USSR and the USA in this respect.[29] However, the essential difference is that in the USA the laws against homosexuality are rarely applied, whereas in the USSR those who have been corrupted in prison are afterwards persecuted, if they cannot divest themselves of homosexual tendencies, by the very authorities who are responsible for their condition.

8

Bribery

Bribery is common to all mankind, though it is more prevalent in some countries than others, and many different methods have been tried to persuade persons in authority to bend the rules in favor of private interests. Bribery was notoriously widespread in pre-Revolutionary Russia,* and when workers', peasants', and soldiers' deputies came to power they found that their own State apparatus was not exempt from it. At the outset this could be blamed on "capitalist elements," but, as the Soviet jurist I. P. Kucheryavy observed, the less enlightened or conscientious elements of the working class were quick to follow suit. "However," he hastened to add, "the venality of members of the working class was different in principle, as it sprang from different causes. They committed this crime because of ignorance and the survival of capitalist ideas and outworn notions concerning the State and its servants."[1]

The new regime's first decree against bribery[2] made a

* An article by A. Estrin in the Soviet *Encyclopedia of State and Law* draws attention to the old Muscovite term *kormlenie* ("feeding"), which indicated that officials were not paid a salary but were expected to "live off the job"; this they did by extracting every penny they could from those who were obliged to have dealings with them.

distinction between whether the offense was committed by workers or "capitalist elements": "If a person guilty of offering or accepting bribes belongs to the property-owning class and makes use of the bribe to preserve or secure privileges connected with the right of property, he shall be sentenced to the most unpleasant form of hard labor and all his property shall be confiscated." Apart from this, the minimum sentence for bribery was five years' hard labor. The law prescribed no maximum, and sentences at that period ranged up to ten years or even death by shooting.* In 1922 the Criminal Code of the RSFSR enacted the death penalty for bribery with aggravating circumstances.

There is plenty of evidence of bribery in the early years of the Soviet regime. In 1922 Felix Dzerzhinsky, then People's Commissar for Communications, observed: "We are all well aware how prevalent bribery has become in many branches of our economic life." Some improvement was achieved by savage punishments and periodic purges of the administration; but at the end of the 1930s, when one might think that "capitalist elements" had been wiped out and when socialism had officially triumphed in the USSR, the fight against bribery was still a live issue. Kucheryavy[3] explained this in 1957 by saying that "the building of socialism in our country did not mean that all Soviet citizens were thenceforth actuated by a socialist conscience. As we know, people's consciousness tends to lag behind their actual situation. Thus individual Soviet citizens living in a socialist society retained in their mental make-up survivals of the old order and the ideology of private capitalism."

* Capital punishment for bribery is not a novelty in history. Herodotus relates that the Persian king Cambyses had a venal judge executed and upholstered the judicial bench with his skin. The law of Twelve Tables in ancient Rome prescribed the death sentence for a judge who took bribes, though nothing was said about officials. According to Estrin's article in the *Encyclopedia of State and Law*, Peter the Great also invoked the death penalty against bribery.

At the present time Soviet ideologists still recognize the persistence of such survivals in individual citizens, and it would indeed be difficult to account in any other way for the continued prevalence of the capitalist crime of bribery.

Under present Soviet criminal legislation, an official who takes a bribe is liable to imprisonment for three to ten years with confiscation of property. If there are aggravating circumstances, the punishment is eight to fifteen years, with or without subsequent exile, with confiscation of property. Aggravating circumstances are the responsible position of the guilty party, a previous conviction for the same offense, or demanding or receiving bribes on more than one occasion. In the case of especially aggravating circumstances— the law does not say what these are—the penalty is death and confiscation of property.

For being an intermediary in cases of bribery (again the law does not define this crime) the penalty is from two to eight years' imprisonment or, if there are aggravating circumstances, from seven to fifteen years, with or without subsequent confiscation of property.

The person who bribes an official is liable to imprisonment of from three to eight years. In the case of a previous conviction or a multiple offense, the penalty is imprisonment of from seven to fifteen years with or without subsequent exile and with or without confiscation of property.*
However, the giver of a bribe is not held criminally responsible if he acted under coercion, or if having given a bribe, he voluntarily reported the fact.

Severe as the Soviet penal code is in general, it seems especially so as regards bribery. Whether this reduces the

---

* It is noteworthy that in the present Criminal Code the maximum penalty for giving a bribe is less than for receiving one. In the Criminal Code of 1926 the maximum for receiving a bribe (without aggravating circumstances) was two years, while for giving a bribe it was five years.

incidence of bribery or only the number of prosecutions for it is hard to say. The severity of the punishment causes potential offenders to exercise caution and often deters potential plaintiffs: not everyone wants to see the death penalty or a long term of imprisonment inflicted on someone who, like many others, accepts a reward for helping individuals to settle their affairs. Even if the plaintiff is not deterred by humanitarian considerations, he has his own interest to bear in mind. He may be exempt from criminal responsibility if he reports the bribe, but he loses the benefit in return for which the bribe was given.* This must tend to diminish the number of those who report bribes. However, an investigator who lacks evidence against a particular official will often try to persuade suspected bribers to come forward by promising them exemption if they do so. This may well be necessary, as venal officials take care to cover their tracks, and it is often hard to find witnesses other than those who have actually given bribes.†

Pre-Revolutionary law distinguished two forms of bribery: *mzdoimstvo* and *likhoimstvo*, which may for convenience be translated as "bribery" and "corruption," respectively. The former consisted of government or public officials taking rewards for performing acts within the area of their competence which were not contrary to their official duties. The penalty for so doing was no more than a

* One might think that a person who voluntarily reports that he has given a bribe, whether in money or in valuables, would get it back, and there is a decision to this effect by the Presidium of the Supreme Court.[4] The 1971 *Commentary*,[5] however, takes a different view.

† A frequent method of detecting bribery is for a *provocateur*—generally an active member of a "social organization"—to pay an official with bills whose numbers have been recorded; the official is then searched and convicted of the crime. In the hope of mitigating the consequences for himself, he is likely to confess and give names of others from whom he has taken bribes. Evidence for use in court can then be obtained from these people, and the part played by the *provocateur* need not be disclosed.

fine. If, however, the acts were contrary to the official's duty, this constituted "corruption," and the penalty was considerably greater.[6]

Soviet law does not distinguish between the two offenses in this way, nor does it prescribe different penalties according to whether the act performed in return for a bribe is in itself legitimate or not. Yet if a citizen is placed by the State in a position where he can secure his legal rights and interests only by bribery, then surely it is not he who is guilty, but rather the State that makes him dependent on a venal official.

If, on the other hand, a person bribes an official to commit an illegal act, there is a criminal conspiracy, and it would seem that the briber's responsibility should be related to the nature of the act in question. However, in a country like the USSR, where the laws and regulations governing the State's relations with its citizens are not fully disclosed to the public, it can and often does happen that the offerer of a bribe believes that the service he is seeking in return is in accordance with his legal rights and interests, while the official concerned knows from unpublished instructions that higher authority has decided against the satisfaction of the citizen's request, lawful as it may seem. For instance, the law guarantees that a citizen of the USSR has the right to choose his place of residence,[7] but in practice he can do so only with the consent of the local police. Since the grounds on which the police do or do not issue a residence permit have never been fully published,* a citizen may apply in good faith for permission to live in a certain city, while the police refuse his request in accordance with their general instructions. These are often loosely formulated, however, so that a police officer may grant the individual's request without committing a serious misdemeanor, and sometimes

* A recent Order by the Council of Ministers of the USSR[8] is entitled "Some [sic] Rules concerning the Registration of Citizens."

he is persuaded to do so by means of a bribe; evidence indicates that this happens frequently.

As registration is generally a matter for the police, not many cases of this sort are discussed in juridical literature. Criminologists are careful not to encourage the public to form prejudices against the authorities. Many people have trouble over residence permits, and there is much talk of the regulations being circumvented by bribery; the authorities naturally do not wish to add fuel to the flames by publishing accounts that would confirm the general suspicion.

In the chapter on hooliganism I pointed out that Soviet legislation tends to avoid defining offenses as precisely as could be wished; this is equally true of bribery, even though a death sentence may be involved. The law does not define what a bribe is but declares in the broadest terms that it is a punishable offense to give or receive "a bribe in any form for the performance or nonperformance of any act, in the interests of the person offering the bribe, which an official should or might commit by virtue of his position."

The courts interpret bribery in a wide sense. In principle, a benefit of any kind may be regarded as a bribe, though recently the tendency appears to be to confine it to material benefits or their equivalent. In the 1920s, however, there were cases of a woman's favors being treated as a bribe. The Supreme Court of the Ukraine declared in 1924 that the object of a person receiving or demanding bribes might be "to satisfy his needs with money or food and other material things, or to gratify his sexual needs and receive physical pleasure in one form or another."[9] An article published in *Pravo i Zhizn* (Law and Life) in 1925 stated:

> The recognition that a woman's offering her body may be a form of bribery should be instructive to both sexes. If she does so to persuade an official to commit an offense, and he in fact enjoys her favors, he is

guilty of accepting a bribe. In this way antisocial and criminal acts not expressly envisaged by the Criminal Code can be brought within its purview. Meanwhile, until this view is generally accepted, such acts can be classified as bribery by analogy.[10]

However, the Supreme Court of the RSFSR did not go so far. In 1927 it laid down that "if a woman gives herself to an official in the hope of being awarded judgment in a matter within his jurisdiction, this does not constitute a crime."[11]

Most Soviet jurists seem to agree that a clearly nonmaterial benefit such as favorable press review[12] cannot be regarded as a bribe. Opinions vary, however, as to material objects of value to the receiver only, for example, a photograph or a private letter.[13]*

In addition to money and other material objects, Soviet practice regards any material benefits as capable of constituting a bribe. In 1929 the Plenum of the Supreme Court of the USSR ruled that "all forms of entertainment offered to an official in return for services are to be classed as a bribe."[15]

Various forms of pluralism are widely regarded as bribery in Soviet judicial practice—e.g., if a person works for two institutions that have business relations, and also various ways of requiting favors performed by officials, even though in many cases those offering the reward are themselves officials and stand to gain no personal advantage from resorting to "legal forms of bribery." In 1949 the

---

* The 1971 *Commentary* states: "Anything of material value can be a bribe: money, clothes, food, building and other materials, securities, domestic animals, rights and services of a material character: e.g., the transferring of rights to a garden plot or its temporary use, making clothes, repairing an apartment, arranging admission to a sanatorium. An object or service without material value, e.g., a photograph or drawing or favorable press notice, cannot be considered as a bribe; nor can sexual intercourse."[14]

Plenum of the Supreme Court declared that "courts are sometimes lenient toward officials who offer bribes owing to a false conception of administrative necessity. In taking this attitude the courts underrate the harmfulness and social danger of such crimes."[16]

Given the nature of the Soviet economy, it is clear that the "false conception of administrative necessity" refers to the efforts of directors of enterprises to achieve, by hook or by crook, the smooth and punctual fulfillment of the plan governing production, trade, distribution, etc. The Supreme Court was indeed right to suggest that these men were actuated not simply by public interest but by fear of being prosecuted for inefficiency or even sabotage, especially in the climate of 1949. Five years earlier, a supply official was convicted for giving two liters of oil to a railroad dispatcher who had obliged him by hastening the delivery of two tanks of oil to his department. The sentence was confirmed by the Plenum of the Supreme Court.[17]

In theory and practice, opinions differ as to who is an official for the purpose of the law against bribery. In the 1920s and 1930s the term was applied to civil servants, workers and collective farmers, and once even to a drayman. Later it was generally confined to administrators; but neither the law nor juridical literature provide a list of functions by which an official is to be recognized, or a definition of the term, broad or narrow as the case may be.

In a note to Article 170 (Abuse of Authority or Official Position), the Criminal Code provides a vague indication of who is an official in the context of administrative misdemeanors. It states that the term includes "persons permanently or temporarily performing the functions of representatives of authority, or who, permanently or temporarily, in State or public institutions, organizations or enterprises, perform duties connected with the discharge of administrative, organizational or economic obligations, or who are specially empowered to discharge such obligations, in the said institutions, organizations and enterprises."

By the letter of the law a private person cannot be convicted of bribery, as the article in question figures under "Administrative Crimes," and Soviet jurists are generally agreed that these can be committed only by officials. A bribe, it would seem, can only be offered by an official for a purpose connected with his official duties: for instance, it would not be a bribe if a private person gave money to a stationmaster to allow him to go to the head of the line for tickets, or if an official did the same thing when going on a private trip. Unfortunately, in practice, no defense can be founded on these arguments.*

Soviet jurists in fact hold that the giving of bribes, or acting as an intermediary therein, is "essentially" not an administrative crime,[18] and that if these acts figure in the "Administrative" section of the Code, it is only to suit the legislators' desire for convenient arrangement.

To all appearances, bribery is extremely widespread in the Soviet Union. The following examples are taken from the records of the Supreme Court of the RSFSR for 1964–72.[19]

Yerofeykin, a printer, took bribes from graduate students for printing, out of turn, the theses they were due to defend

---

* The Criminal Code of the RSFSR is customarily referred to as law, and I have followed this practice here and elsewhere; but it has not in fact been adopted as a law in conformity with the RSFSR Constitution. In 1960 the Supreme Soviet of the USSR adopted a law of the RSFSR "Confirming the Criminal Code of the RSFSR," but it did not describe the Code as a law of the RSFSR. This peculiar legislative technique is employed by the Supreme Soviet of the USSR and the Supreme Soviets of the constituent Soviet Republics when adopting, or rather confirming, many legal instruments which are then themselves supposed to be laws. In particular, decrees issued by the Presidiums of the Supreme Soviets are customarily regarded as having force of law after, or even before, they are confirmed by the enactment of a law by the Supreme Soviet in question.

at the customary oral examination. This is a typical occurrence, as delay in printing complicates the already laborious process of preparing to defend one's thesis.

Kazakov and Gurenkova, electrical inspectors in the Kaliningrad region, found that in some houses appliances were wired in such a way that the electricity consumed was not recorded on the meter. Instead of having the occupants fined, they accepted a 20-ruble bribe from each offender.

Zhurova, a housing officer in Leningrad, took bribes for helping individuals obtain and exchange accommodations.

Levit, an instructor at a Leningrad automobile club, took 5 rubles from each applicant for a license for letting them see the test questions in advance; altogether he received 1,125 rubles.

Rankov, manager of a store in Leningrad, took bribes for letting citizens buy imported furniture out of turn.

Erblat, a woman doctor at the Leningrad gynecological hospital, took bribes for performing abortions, contrary to the regulations, on patients who had not been referred to her by the Woman's Clinic. (Women evidently avoid being certified by the clinic for the same reasons that they have abortions outside the hospital; as I mentioned earlier, the lack of medical secrecy in the USSR is a factor leading to crime in this area.)

Inspectors in the Buriat republic discovered irregularities on the part of the shopkeepers and used the threat of exposure to extort bribes.

A secretary-typist at a technical school in the Chelyabinsk region accepted rewards for using her position to help applicants for admission to the school. The court ruled that the nature of her work made her an official.

Paramonov, the curator of a Leningrad cemetery, accepted through a gravedigger a bribe of 150 rubles from a man who wished to select a different plot than the one proposed for his wife's grave.

In a case tried by the Supreme Court of the RSFSR,[20] two officials bribed each other. Zavgorodnyaya, secretary of the extension course division of a university, obtained an apartment through the good offices of Tetera, housing inspector under the local Executive Committee, and in return faked the latter's record of university grades. They received sentences of eight and three years respectively.

It is fairly common for people to bribe their way into universities. A frequent subterfuge is for a dishonest lecturer or member of the admissions board to give the aspiring student private lessons for a large fee. Sometimes the desire of young people to get into a university is exploited by swindlers who pretend to be able to help them through influence or to bribe the examiners. When they have extorted money and the candidate fails the exam, they tell the parents that it is no good reporting the matter to the authorities, since the parents themselves would get into trouble for attempted bribery. Other, more ingenious rogues promise to return the bribe if the candidate is unsuccessful. This they do, but as some candidates get in on their own merits, the swindler can still make a handsome profit.

In general, the prevalence of bribery in Russia is accentuated by the fact that many goods are in short supply and are distributed in accordance with an elaborate network of privileges. Since people cannot buy wanted items in the usual way, they have to bribe those who control the privilege system. For instance, some goods, including certain foodstuffs, can be bought only in special shops from exclusive distributors; for some films, especially foreign ones, tickets are sold only to a privileged public; to go to a holiday resort one must be a shock worker or an especially needy case, or get the blessings of one's trade union chiefs. In some cases the privilege is geographical: items that can be bought freely in Moscow are often in short supply in the provinces, and storekeepers may decide to use them to curry favor with local authorities rather than sell them to the general public. In these and many other cases, bribery is the only way of by-passing the system of overt and clandestine privilege.

9

Private Enterprise

As a rule, Soviet criminologists' and ideologists' fondness for attributing crime to "survivals of capitalist mentality" must provoke an ironical smile. It is justified, however, in the case of private enterprise, which is, of course, a crime only in Soviet eyes.

The survival of this "deviation" means, first and foremost, that people continue to insist on their right to pursue normal human interests and refuse to allow all of their economic dealings to be subject to totalitarian regulation in the name of socialism. In this sense, private enterprise is merely a holdover from the presocialist way of life. What Soviet ideologists call capitalism is not a social system based on a particular doctrine, but simply the natural form of economic dealings in which the free initiative of every participant is limited by the State only so far as is necessary to protect the freedom of others.

As soon as the Bolsheviks came to power, they declared war on the bourgeoisie and on private enterprise; they confiscated large and small businesses* and proclaimed a State

---

* This confiscation was called nationalization, but I prefer not to use this term since it may suggest wrongly that compensation was paid to the owners, as is customary when enterprises are nationalized.

monopoly of all aspects of economic life. In 1922, there was an armistice—Lenin's New Economic Program—when economic chaos forced the new rulers to tolerate some forms of private enterprise. However, they made it clear that this was only a temporary and tactical retreat. By the end of the 1920s, when the economy, thanks largely to private enterprise, had somewhat recovered, the State resumed its monopoly.

Today, after decades of terror, the authorities have achieved more or less full control over the economy and over jobs. Nonetheless, the memory of the older way of life is still strong in the public mind, and a surprising amount of private initiative persists, especially in trade and small-scale enterprise. At times one even hears of illegal privately owned factories or the creation of a "private sector" within a State enterprise. To assess the strength of the "survival of a capitalist mentality" one should take into account not only the people who carry on such activity but also those who take advantage of the goods and services it offers. Both groups are numerous; in fact there is scarcely a person in the Soviet Union who has not at some time bought goods from a speculator or a craftsman engaged in illegal industry.

Only some forms of economic initiative are criminal offenses in the Soviet Union. I am concerned with those activities that the State could permit without any serious damage to its monopoly, and that would indeed increase the welfare of working people and help to satisfy their "growing cultural and material demands." These include certain industries, petty trading (at present condemned as speculation), commercial brokerage, and even some forms of what the Criminal Code calls "private enterprise exploiting State, cooperative, and other social forms." I would not presume to say how far official toleration of these activities would be consistent with socialist ideology; but East European countries that call themselves socialist permit private enterprise on a much wider scale than is allowed in the Soviet Union. This may, of course, merely signify that these countries have advanced less far on the road toward socialist and Communist ideals. Nevertheless it is interesting that the Soviet historian, Roy Medvedev, who criticizes many of the Soviet rulers' acts from a Communist point of view, states that "Marxism . . . has never asserted that there can be no private economic initiative in a socialist society and that all small private enterprises and *artels*, including those providing services, must be forbidden."[1]

In March 1971 the Nobel Prize-winning scientist Andrei Sakharov addressed a memorandum to Brezhnev urging, among other things, "increased opportunities and facilities for private initiative in service enterprises, medical care, small-scale trading, education, etc."* From time to time even official Soviet publications suggest, in a less outspoken way, that restrictions on private enterprise might be relaxed.

Under Soviet law it is a crime or a misdemeanor (*delikt*) for a private person to engage in a "prohibited industry." A list of such industries was given in a government order of 1949,[2] which has been amended and supplemented several times since. In 1965, certain private industries or crafts connected with consumer goods were permitted outside of Moscow and Leningrad: these include repairing overshoes and other rubber footwear, the manufacturing and selling of clothespins, making hats, carpets, and rugs from customers' material, and a few more. In rural areas it has become lawful for private individuals to repair television sets, watches, fountain pens, etc., and to set up shop as a blacksmith, hairdresser, or manicurist. Special concessions have been given to the aged and to disabled veterans.

* *Sakharov Speaks* (New York, 1974), p. 146.

Even before 1965 some private enterprise was permitted, such as sawing and cutting wood, washing windows and floors, polishing shoes, and making knickknacks out of wood, bone, stone, clay, and straw. It was forbidden, on the other hand, to make metal bedsteads, carpets or rugs from material woven by home workers, to process woolen yarn, to set oneself up as a tailor or dressmaker, to make objects from nonferrous metals, from leather or from rubber. It was also forbidden to process foodstuffs or to manufacture notebooks, envelopes, packages, mirrors, and candles.

Special prohibitions still apply to the printing industry and the production of duplicating machines, dies, stamps, and typewriters. These, of course, are connected with the control of information as well as with the government's economic monopoly. In the same way, the prohibition of the private manufacture of full-length veils and *yashmaks* in the Uzbek republic[3] is no doubt socially as well as economically motivated, since use of these items is associated with the Uzbeks' Moslem tradition.

The penalty for engaging in a prohibited industry, without aggravating circumstances, is at present fairly lenient: a fine of 200 rubles (about 275 dollars) or up to a year's correctional labor without deprivation of freedom. If there are aggravating circumstances, such as employment of hired labor, a previous conviction, or production on a large scale,* the penalty may be as much as four years' imprisonment, with or without confiscation of property. (Confiscation includes both the items produced and the means of production.)

As an example of what the law considers profit on a large scale, let us take the case of Grigoryev and Sobolev[5] (reported in the collected proceedings of the Supreme Court)

---

* The 1971 *Commentary*[4] on the Criminal Code states that evidence of large-scale activity may be the quantity of production, the amount of profit, the number of hands employed, or the period of time involved.

who bought television sets and resold them at a profit of 50 to 60 rubles each. Sobolev resold fifteen sets in the years 1964–67, and Grigoryev, ten in 1965–67. They thus netted less than 200 rubles a year or about 20 rubles a month. Unskilled Soviet workers are paid 60 rubles a month or more, yet these men were convicted for carrying on prohibited activity on a large scale.

In some cases the court's finding lays more emphasis on sale than on production, and the offender is convicted under Article 154 forbidding speculation. For example, a man who bought piglets, fattened them up and sold them at a profit,[6] was convicted of speculation even though he had invested his own labor and paid for the fodder.*

If goods are bought, subjected to what the courts consider inessential changes, and then resold, Soviet law considers this speculation, not industry. The *Commentary*[7] quotes the case of a person buying tulle and making curtains out of it. Making curtains is a prohibited industry in the USSR and people have been convicted for it.[8] The *Commentary*, no doubt in accordance with judicial practice, classifies the case quoted as one of speculation, for no apparent reason except, perhaps, that speculation carries a heavier punishment (imprisonment for a maximum of seven years) than illegal production.

Article 9 of the Soviet Constitution states that "alongside the socialist system, which is the dominant form of the economy of the USSR, the law permits small-scale private economic activity by individual peasants and craftsmen, based on their own labor and without the exploitation of others' labor." It might seem that this provision, and the legal guarantee of the right to choose one's own occupation (Article 9 of the Fundamentals of Civil Legislation), grant the Soviet citizen considerable scope to exercise private

* Notes of the *All-Union Institute of Legal Science* (1957), No. 2, p. 28.

initiative and that the penalties laid down in the Criminal Code for engaging in prohibited industries are intended only to protect public safety and the rights of others. Typically, however, the list of such prohibited industries is contained not in the law but in an administrative order and is by no means confined to such threats to the public safety as the manufacture of explosives.

Since criminal sanctions can be imposed only in accordance with the law, it would seem that, as a matter of legal principle, the legislature should not allow penalties to be attached to a catalog of offenses it has not itself drawn up. However, in the Soviet Union, this is by no means the case. One might suppose, on the basis of the law, that a prohibited industry is one there is good reason to keep out of private hands, e.g., on the grounds of safety. In point of fact, it is prohibited to make envelopes or to buy and restore old furniture for resale at a profit.

Soviet jurists defend the wholesale restriction of crafts on both economic and ideological grounds. Professor A. A. Pointkovsky declared in the 1950s that the object of the law was to protect the Soviet economy and that engaging in prohibited industry "impeded the development of the corresponding sectors of the State economy." This seems to suggest that cottage industry offers serious competition to State industry and the cooperative economy. I am no expert in economics, but surely undertakings based on large-scale investment and turnover have an advantage over small craftsmen. The Soviet authorities themselves attribute the development of monopolies in the capitalist system to the advantages of scale. But in a socialist economy perhaps things work differently, and the cottage industries have really proved to be a threat to State industries. Still, it is hard to believe that objects produced singly by craftsmen can be serious competition to mass-produced goods. Furthermore the craftsman generally pays close attention to the market and does not waste his time making things that can easily be found in the shops: he concentrates on items that are in short supply. In this fashion resourceful individuals help to overcome shortages caused by the inadequate production or faulty distribution of State enterprises.

A recent book* reports the case of a group of female "criminals" engaged in making nylon blouses: "They then switched their activity to making perlon blouses, converting imported men's shirts into women's blouses, and speculating in knitwear. . . . This brazen, organized activity was made possible by the lack of initiative of the directors of light industry and retail establishments who failed to anticipate customers' needs and demand, and also by the inefficiency of the local police department whose duty it was to combat such violations but who failed to put a timely stop to the criminal enterprise of V. and her associates."

These women's activity, as long as it lasted, benefited their customers, and one result of the court's observations on the causes of their crime was that "the directors of consumer goods plants paid more attention to satisfying customers' demand." It would seem that the upshot of the whole affair was beneficial to Soviet industry.

Such examples show that home workers not only do not compete with socialist industry but perform a useful function by satisfying demand and, if they are detected and convicted, by exposing deficiencies in the public sector which can then be remedied.

In one field private enterprise does indeed seem to compete with the socialist economy, and that is in the provision of services. In 1973 *Literaturnaya Gazeta* (The Literary Gazette, a Moscow weekly) published an article on the deficiencies of the State organization *Zarya* (Dawn), which is supposed to be in charge of the finishing touches on

---

* N. Sokolov and I. Chupalenkov, *The Soviet Court* (Moscow, 1973), p. 34.

houses in new settlements;[9] the author complained that it did its work so badly, for instance in insulating doors to keep out the winter cold, that people had no choice but to call in spare-time workers (*shabashniki*). In a subsequent issue[10] the journal published, surprisingly enough, an unsigned letter from a team of *shabashniki*, who said that organizations like *Zarya* had never competed seriously with them. "When we look in at a new home, the *Zarya* people are nowhere. Our leatherette is better than theirs at the same price, we always have locks and doorhandles and peepholes ready for fitting, and we fix the doors better and cheaper than they do. We charge more only if we do some extra job like installing a heater. . . . You think it is shocking that we go to work in decent clothes—actually in winter we put on work clothes like anyone else, but a man is judged by his appearance, and people would sooner deal with us than with some drunken, unshaven fuddy-duddy who sticks his nose into the apartment and says, 'I'm from *Zarya*; do you want your door fixed up?' What matters to the customer is not whether it's us or *Zarya*, but who does the job better." The writers go on to say that they are college graduates but are paid only 120–140 rubles a month as junior technicians; they can't live on less than 500–600, and they make up the rest "in the sweat of our brow, by the work of our own hands."

The phenomenon of a university graduate doing odd jobs in his spare time is a new one in the USSR; it is increasing, and seems likely to go on doing so. Many are intelligent, resourceful young people who find to their chagrin that higher education has not done them any good materially. As electricians, radio technicians, or locksmiths they were able to earn quite good money in factories or research institutions, especially if they took on more than one job. Then they went to night school or enrolled in an extension course, got a degree, and found that as junior engineers they were earning much less than as skilled workmen. Naturally such people put their talents to work by earning extra money in their spare time. They are also ready to change jobs promptly if there proves to be no demand for their services, or if they are poorly treated. The above-quoted letter continues: "Bear in mind that if we are not allowed to fix people's doors, flooring, etc. (just as we were once warned off photography), we shall find something else to do. Initiative, resource, inventiveness, and business sense pay off quickly, and very well, too. That's why we *shabashniki* are on top, and always will be, as far as household services and new kinds of work are concerned. We don't have to fill in a thousand forms before we are allowed to drive in a nail or to adopt new specifications."

To justify the restrictions imposed upon private industry, Soviet authors often point out that such work involves misappropriation of socialist property. So it does, but only because, thanks to restrictions, materials cannot be bought in the ordinary way, and the craftsman has either to buy them from middlemen, who steal them from State factories, or steal them himself. Most people would doubtless prefer to buy their necessary supplies honestly, but the State makes this impossible. For instance, one cannot buy leather to make shoes, upholster chairs, or bind books. So when a man is charged with making shoes illegally, he is usually also charged with stealing leather from the State—an excellent example of how, by prohibiting a harmless activity, the State incites people to commit more serious offenses.

There are, of course, also ideological arguments against private enterprise. The 1964 *Commentary on the Criminal Code of the RSFSR*[11] states that engaging in prohibited industry tends to develop habits and attitudes characteristic of a system of private property. No doubt it does, but surely the State was aware of this when it enacted the Constitution which guarantees peasants and craftsmen the right to engage in small-scale economic activities. It would be ridiculous to suggest that some industries encourage capitalist habits and attitudes and others do not, especially as one would then have to explain why making clothespins, for example, originally had this harmful quality but apparently later lost it, since it was removed from the prohibited list in 1965.

Sometimes Soviet authorities defend the restrictions on economic grounds. The six-volume textbook *Course of Soviet Criminal Law*,[12] edited by a group of eminent jurists, states that "engaging in prohibited industry impairs the efficient economic use of productive forces and the means and instruments of production and prevents the output of Soviet industry from providing the optimum satisfaction of the needs of society." It still does not make clear why the private manufacture of clothespins was a wasteful use of productive forces up to 1965 and not afterwards, but perhaps the Council of Ministers of the USSR was simply rectifying a mistake.

Cottage industry by its very nature is to some extent contrary to what Soviet economists and ideologists understand as the efficient use of productive forces. Every individual craftsman, unless he is disabled or of pensionable age, is a potential member of the socialist economy who for some reason prefers to work on his own. And although the analysis of these reasons is a matter for investigation by Soviet experts, it is not hard to guess at what some of them must be—the desire to display initiative, a preference for organizing one's own schedule, dislike of having one's labor and conduct regulated by a boss—in short, "habits and attitudes characteristic of the system of private property."

Ideology apart, there are obvious economic objections from the authorities' point of view to private enterprise becoming widespread among the population. But is such work really so profitable or appealing that, if the restrictions were removed, everyone in the country would rush to engage in a one-man business? *The Course of Soviet Criminal Law*[13] says that "it is recognized as socially dangerous to permit industries that may involve large profits"; and perhaps this is the nub of the official objection. Private industry often performs a useful function in satisfying demand for goods and services that the socialist economy is unable to meet; but if it offers the hope of profits on a larger scale than the socialist wage for doing the same job, there is a risk that many skilled craftsmen will be tempted into the private sector, to the detriment of the "efficient use of productive forces." The authors of the *Course* go on to say frankly: "It is rightly pointed out in legal literature that when craftsmen, technicians, workers, and officials engage in prohibited industries in their spare time, their activity is socially dangerous inasmuch as they lose interest in socialist output, thus diminishing the productivity of labor in socialist enterprises."

It may be asked why the State could not remove many occupations from the prohibited list while imposing taxes on profits so that private craftsmen receive no more for their labor than workers in socialist industry. The authors quoted say, however, that "it is not possible to ensure by taxation that the surplus product is devoted to satisfying the needs of the whole of society."

"Private enterprise making use of State, cooperative, or other social forms" (Article 153 of the Criminal Code) is another form of activity subject to criminal sanctions. The maximum sentence is five years' imprisonment with confiscation of property.

As in many other cases, the offense is not defined as precisely as one might wish. Only by study of judicial practice can one get an idea of how judges interpret "State, cooperative, or other social forms."

In the late 1920s the authorities fought so-called bogus cooperatives, that is, attempts by capitalist elements to carry on private enterprise under cover of the cooperative system permitted by the Soviet government. According to the 1971 *Commentary*[14] the "use of State, cooperative, or other social forms" may consist of the following:

> "(a) giving a private enterprise the appearance of a socialist organization (pseudo enterprise, pseudo cooperative) or the appearance of a separate unit of an actually existing socialist enterprise (pseudo workshop, pseudo branch);
> "(b) carrying on unrecorded production within a socialist enterprise for the purpose of private profit."

This sheds little light on the meaning of "State and social forms," but it shows the types of illicit private enterprise met with in judicial practice. It should not be assumed, however, that these are the only cases in which Soviet courts would apply the law in question.

It is difficult to say how prevalent the offense is. Soviet publications seldom mention pseudo enterprises or pseudo workshops, perhaps for fear of putting ideas into people's heads. Occasionally, however, such activities are reported. We read, for instance, in M. G. Lyubarsky's book *How Secrets Are Discovered* (Leningrad, 1968) of a Leningrad lawyer[15] who set up a shoe-making organization and arranged the sale of its products through a shoestore. And the newspaper *Eastern Dawn* for September 8, 1972, reports on a Georgian named Barabadze[16] who ran an underground distillery turning out adulterated brandy. Given the strict internal passport and labor regulations and the abundance of informers in Russia, it cannot be easy to organize a clandestine enterprise, but evidently some people are resourceful enough to do so.

The commonest form of the offense seems to be unregistered production within a State enterprise. Those who are brought to book for such activities are generally also charged with stealing socialist property and abusing their official position. Minor cases appear to be frequent and are not always easy to uncover; for example, when a group of workers fills private orders for goods or manufactures them for sale on the premises of a socialist enterprise. For this they do not need to organize a pseudo workshop; the offense may be committed by a single individual. Indeed a dental technician named Rezvov, employed at an out-patient clinic, was sentenced under Article 153 by the Supreme Court for manufacturing false teeth on a private basis.[17]

It is risky to try to organize such activity on a large scale because of the number of potential informers, but in Georgia and the other southern republics, where people are less apt to betray one another to the authorities, pseudo workshops and even pseudo businesses are not uncommon. In the 1960s there were unofficial reports that a network of clandestine organizations involving several branches of industry had been discovered in Kirgizia, complete with its own equipment, production and marketing arrangements, accounting system, and distribution of profits.

Those who control the Soviet economy no doubt recognize the strength of the acquisitive instinct, but they try to channel all economic initiative into the direct service of the State. In the last few decades, however, they have begun to see the advantage of allowing individual citizens a material interest, as they call it, in the prosperity of the State. The Liberman economic reform, introduced experimentally on a limited test basis in 1964, provided for some decentralization of economic decisions, production keyed to demand, and "profit" incentives, thus encouraging initiative on the part of managers. The Liberman reform was shelved in the late 1960s, partly because the authorities feared the managers of State enterprises would take advantage of the increased opportunities offered for graft and embezzlement. Considering the amount of corruption under the prevailing system of strict controls, perhaps those fears are justified.

Some Soviet publications suggest that decentralization has not been more successful because of the laws restricting the search for new and freer forms of enterprise. A Moscow lawyer, V. Ya. Shveisky, drew attention to this problem after he had been involved in a complicated case. The managers of a design office, organized in 1965 under DOSAAF (the Voluntary Society for Aid to the Soviet Armed Forces), were prosecuted for economic crimes. Shveisky describes the outcome of the Office's activity as follows:

> At the time when this organization wound up, it had completed experimental and other operations under twenty-eight research contracts relating to underwater structures and to scientific research conducted underwater. This activity had been perfectly overt, and it was clear that the organization was creating new forms of voluntary cooperation which improved our country's ability to solve important scientific and economic problems.

Nevertheless, its operations were found to be illegal because its balance sheet was not registered with the financial authorities, and the organization was consequently not subject to financial control. Instead of having an organization bank account, the director opened several savings accounts in his own name. The sums the organization received in payment for its work went into these accounts, and he settled with the research workers who did the work according to his own judgment, there being no approved estimates. It turned out that contracts were signed for work that had nothing to do with underwater exploration, and fictitious accounts came into being. Several of those involved were found guilty of embezzlement. The case was described by

Shveisky in the *Literary Gazette*[18] and was also the subject of an article in *Izvestia*.[19]

The courts often have to deal with unlawful initiative by managers of State enterprises carrying out the State Plan, and it is noteworthy that in many cases the activities for which they are condemned do not involve any direct personal profit to themselves. (The annual State Plan establishes strict production goals and also payroll, investment, supply, and other budgets for each enterprise. The director is responsible for the fulfillment of the Plan by his group.) As a matter of practical experience, the production goals of the Plan for an enterprise often cannot be fulfilled on schedule without violating the detailed prescriptions of the Plan for payroll, etc., or committing some other illegal act such as bribery to procure needed supplies. The head of a building firm, for example, complained that the only way he could get an allocation for the necessary labor force to build a bridge was to fool the authorities by including the construction of a school in his Plan and then diverting some of the workers from that project to bridge building. Directors often cut corners and use reciprocal favors or bribes to get raw materials on time; the authorities usually turn a blind eye to this "for the good of the cause," but from time to time they or the courts remind the executives that the law must not be broken even for the sake of fulfilling the Plan. The executives for their part are well aware that it is impossible to carry on business without transgressing the detailed restrictions imposed from above.

Like other aspects of criminal law, the ban on private enterprise may be used by the authorities as a means of ideological pressure. This sometimes happens, for instance, in connection with lectures given by members of the intelligentsia to large audiences at clubs of various kinds. The organizers may violate "financial discipline" by failing to account to the State for the revenue from the sale of tickets for these and similar "cultural events"; the lecturer is usually not in a position to know whether the regulations have been observed, but if the organizers are found guilty he may be held criminally responsible for taking part in an enterprise for private gain, even though he had no idea that anything untoward was going on. Two cases of this sort have come to light recently. The first was that of Mikhail Kalik, a film director, who, like many others, lectured to clubs and showed excerpts from his films. Unfortunately he had got on the wrong side of the authorities by applying for permission to emigrate to Israel. He was threatened with prosecution for illegal enterprise. Fortunately, the prosecution was dropped after pressure from abroad, and Kalik was allowed to leave the USSR.

The second case had a less happy ending. Eduard Naumov, a student of parapsychology, was sentenced in 1974 to two years' imprisonment for "engaging in private enterprise": he had given lectures to several clubs at their invitation, and in one case the organizers did not record the proceeds from admissions accurately. They were declared nonaccountable because of mental illness and confined in psychiatric hospitals, but Naumov was convicted by the court although, according to his statement, he firmly believed that all the formalities had been properly carried out. During the trial he told the court: "I must say that I have never heard of a lecturer concerning himself with who hires the hall and what it costs, or who the film projectionists and cleaners and cloakroom attendants are." Naumov's lawyer, Dina Kaminskaya, appealed the case to the Moscow City Court, which confirmed the sentence. Many unofficial observers thought the entire affair was part of a campaign to discourage the study of parapsychology. Naumov made a veiled reference to this in court: "When I was interviewed at a certain institution, they asked me whether I thought it was Naumov or parapsychology that was on trial. I do not

want to exaggerate or go in for any more self-advertise-
ment, but I believe all my activity is very closely connected
—all that is happening here is very closely connected with
parapsychology."[20]*

"Speculation," defined as "the purchase and resale of
goods or other articles for gain," is more severely punished
in the Soviet Union than any other form of private enterprise. Legal doctrine and juridical practice regard speculation or trade (an equivalent, but less pejorative term) as a
source of unearned income and thus more reprehensible
than a craftsman's sale of his wares. It is not clear why
commercial profits are regarded as unearned, since they
involve the expenditure of time and effort and a study of the
market. *The Course of Soviet Criminal Law*[21] recognizes
that speculators "take account of seasonal and other factors increasing demand for particular goods in different
localities, and on this basis choose the time and place for
supplying one type of goods and buying another for resale."
However, it is not only jurists who regard the profits of
speculation as unearned; the same opinion is shared by the
Soviet public at large. It may be, of course, that a successful
speculator can make more money than he would in a different form of private industry or, *a fortiori*, in a State enterprise. But for any occupation to be economically worth-
while, its profits must balance the expenditure of capital,
time, labor, and the element of risk—in this case not only
risk due to fluctuations in demand, but also the risk of
prosecution. The penalty for speculation without aggravating circumstances is up to two years' imprisonment and

---

* The source does not make clear what institution Naumov was referring to, but it is highly probable that it was the KGB. There is a psychological taboo against naming this body, and in conversation people
use some well-understood synonym like "the organs" (*organy*), just as
Asiatics and some primitive tribes avoid mentioning the names of persons
who inspire particular respect or fear.

confiscation of property; for large-scale speculation it is up to seven years and confiscation of property. A separate clause provides that a second offense of "petty speculation" is punishable by up to a year's imprisonment. The first such offense is punishable by fine or other disciplinary action.[22] However, the term "petty speculation" is nowhere defined; the courts presumably decide in the light of circumstances and the personality of the accused when speculation on a larger scale is involved.

Only speculators and not their customers are liable to punishment, although *The Course of Soviet Criminal Law*[23] observes that Soviet morality condemns those who make use of the services of speculators. Nevertheless, most people some time do use their services, which does not prevent these very people from using "speculator" as a term of abuse. They object to speculators' unearned profits and exaggerate the ease with which they are made.

Apart from the moral indignation they excite, speculators are often blamed for scarcities which, it is said, they have caused by buying up goods in order to sell them at exorbitant prices. Usually these suspicions are unjustified. Speculators are numerous, but they generally operate singly or in small groups and lack the power to create scarcities of particular items by concerted buying. Shortages usually occur because the State has not produced enough of a commodity to meet demand, or because the retail organizations have not organized sufficient stocks, or, in the case of imported goods, because the foreign-trade organizations have failed to obtain them.

The Course of Soviet Criminal Law[24] states that "speculators frequently deal in goods which are in adequate supply in some areas but not in others." (The respectable Western term for this type of activity is arbitrage.) Sometimes, however, the goods are in short supply everywhere, and this increases the speculator's problems. There are usu-

ally queues in the shops for goods in short supply, and both
shopkeepers and customers keep an eye open for anyone
buying large quantities of them. The amount a single customer can buy is often restricted, so the would-be speculator has to spend a lot of time in queues and thereby runs the
risk of detection. There is, however, an easier way—to
make a private deal with the retailer or his assistants. The
latter are often prosecuted for collusion in cases of major
speculation. Small-scale speculation, on the other hand, is a
matter of opportunity, and many practice it from time to
time: a woman may happen to be in a store when a con-
signment of imported blouses is put on sale; if she has the
money, she may buy one and sell it later to a friend at a
higher price, though this too is against the law.

Another way of speculating in scarce goods is to buy
them from private persons, including foreigners. There is a
special name, *fartsovshchiki*, for those who specialize in
acquiring blue jeans, records, cigarettes, chewing gum, etc.,
in this way.

Most speculators do indeed take advantage of seasonal
and geographical variations of demand and supply, and in
so doing they perform a valuable service. When the government trade organizations fail to distribute goods to the
provinces, speculators, acting at their own risk, cushion the
effects and benefit the local inhabitants as well as themselves. When, as often happens, goods are available in Moscow but not elsewhere, speculators who buy them in
Moscow and resell them in the provinces are countering
geographical discrimination to the best of their ability.

Soviet writers are fairly frank in admitting the causes of
speculation. As one of them observed in *Problems of Crime*
(1972), No. 15:[25] "Just as one cannot at the present time
imagine speculation in matches, soap, sugar, or salt,* so in

---

* This is actually a mistake. There is still speculation in these articles
in some underprivileged areas.

time, as we produce more refrigerators, furs, and building materials, there will no longer be occasion for speculation in these items either."

Numerous as the speculators are, there are not enough of them to counteract all the imbalances in geographical distribution or to correct all the miscalculations of government retail organizations. So huge numbers of provincials flock to Moscow to do their shopping. Sometimes they come from thousands of miles away to buy clothes, toys, household goods, jams, sausages, and confectionery. Some use official trips for this purpose, others spend part of their vacations standing in line in Moscow. Many of these travelers are speculators perforce: the fare is too expensive to make it worth the individual's while to buy goods for his family alone, so he buys as large quantities as possible in order to resell them and recoup his expenses. For doing so he may find himself in court, even though he has not practiced speculation as an industry. Sometimes he may collect orders from his friends and neighbors before setting out for Moscow or some other major city and receive from his customers not only the price of the goods but something extra to cover his travel expenses. In that case he is no longer a mere speculator but a commercial middleman, liable to three years' imprisonment with confiscation of property if the court decides that he was conducting a business or acting for purposes of enrichment. (Some people indeed do precisely this last, and make a very good thing of it.)

Those whose jobs require them to travel frequently—railroad guards, long-distance truck drivers, pilots on civil airlines—form a special class of speculator, operating, as a rule, systematically but on a small scale; the authorities shut their eyes to this, provided it does not go too far.

A large volume could be filled with a list of the items speculators deal in and the areas where they buy and sell them. As far as I know, such a list has never been compiled, which is a pity, as it would tell us a lot about the economic geography of the USSR; it would be instructive not only to speculators but to the State trading organizations. Much information is available in local press reports, however, and to a lesser degree in juridical literature.

Speculation in food items is quite common. According to one source,[26] in a northwestern region of the USSR, in which town dwellers constitute 40 percent of the population, 62 percent of the cases of speculative buying occurred in towns and 38 percent in villages. In the south of Russia proper and in the southern republics, farm products, especially fruit, which is very scarce in the north, are probably a favored object of speculation.

Under Soviet law[27] collective farm workers, self-employed farmers, and all owners of private plots may sell their own products in a raw or processed state; this is virtually the only form of free trade that the law allows. But not all these producers have time to take their goods to market and sell them, and the proceeds often do not repay the journey to a local center, let alone a distant town. Consequently there are people who buy produce from several collective farm workers at a time and sell it in the city, where they hope to obtain a good price. These agents are either speculators, if they first buy the produce and then sell it, or commercial middlemen, if they sell on the producer's behalf and share the profit with him. Both types of "crime" are frequent, especially since the agent may himself be a farm worker who, if questioned, can say that he is only selling his own produce. Thanks to this commercial activity, people in the remotest parts of Russia can buy fruit from the southern republics, while the State distribution system cannot even supply Moscow properly, let alone the far north. True, the price is high, but the people are willing to pay it; they probably realize that the speculator cannot afford to reduce his prices, with transport and packing so expensive and the risk in shipping perishable goods over thousand-mile distances. The speculator makes a profit on the transportation, but his profit can hardly be called unearned.

The authorities are not too hard on small-scale rural speculators, like a southern farm worker who simply takes his own and his neighbor's fruit to market. If they suspect commercial activity on a large scale, they are more likely to prosecute, although in this case, as in many others, the vigilance of the local police depends on the instructions they have received as to the type of crime that has current priority in official campaigns.

Quite a number of fruit speculators seem to operate on a large scale, by Soviet standards at least. In the southern republics a group will sometimes combine to acquire a truck and forge documents for an "official" journey. They risk being stopped and questioned by the police many times en route, but the enterprise is often successful. A Georgian journalist has related how she met such a party, bound for Kuibyshev with a truckload of pears, stuck on a mountain road. She describes their elaborate arrangements:

> These enterprising characters had done their best to ensure success. A short while before, trusted agents with samples of fruit had flown to cities all over the country to see where they could get the best price. Their reports came in by telegram, and the team went into action at once, weighing all the pros and cons and mapping out the route. By five o'clock the next morning they had found a truck, loaded it with peasant produce, organized travel documents in some mysterious way, and begun the wearisome journey over the mountain road. . . . When I met them, they were in a nervous state. What if they couldn't get a tractor to pull the truck out of the mud? A day or two's delay would mean losing tens of thousands of rubles which were

virtually in their pockets. Pears spoil so quickly: delicious fruit one day, and rotten before you know where you are.[28]

The same writer describes how in one night a group of speculators, using a bulldozer, made a private mountain road some hundreds of yards long in order to avoid a police checkpoint. From these and similar accounts, which actually get into the Soviet press, it can be seen that travel expenses absorb a good deal of the speculators' profits, not to speak of the risk they run.

The police take care to see that large quantities of fruit are delivered to storage depots in the south and not sent to other parts of the country. The result is often bad for the fruit as well as the customer: pears and peaches, which spoil easily, frequently find their way from the State distribution centers to nearby jam factories, but seldom to northern towns.

The police are especially vigilant when a republic has not yet fulfilled the State Plan for delivery of a particular kind of fruit. This affects especially citrus fruits produced by collective farm workers or by those with private plots. Speculators do their best, with bribery and ingenuity, to evade the regulations, but they are not always successful. In 1972 the newspaper *Zarya Vostoka* reported that the police had arrested speculators who were driving a truckload of mandarin oranges out of Georgia; they had covered the fruit with a tarpaulin and poured asphalt over it to camouflage their load.

The Soviet press frequently discusses the problem of how to supply the population with cheap fruit and vegetables through the official State distribution system, eliminating private middlemen. The present situation is admitted to be unsatisfactory. One article in *Izvestia* criticized the Leningrad authorities for failing to cope with the storage and sale of even locally grown vegetables[29] and added: "Calculations have shown that even if all vegetables grown in this region were sold to customers, each person would receive tens of pounds less per year than the quantity food experts regard as necessary."

It appears that State trade organizations find it hard to make a profit out of vegetables because prices are fixed at too low a level. This is an economic question, and I cannot discuss it in detail, but the following report gives an idea of how hard it is for the State system to compete with private cultivators and their agents.

A writer in *Izvestia* in 1973 complained[30] that spring vegetables made their first appearance, at a high price, on the open market and not in State shops.

> In Stavropol, a dozen yards from the private market booths, there is a government store with a great sign saying 'Fruit and Vegetables,' but the sign is a lie: the shelves are stacked with canned goods such as cabbage soup. "We do sometimes get fresh vegetables," the senior assistant told me. Twenty steps further on, at City Cooperative No. 7, it's the same story: nothing but piles of cans in the vegetable department.

The reporter made inquiries and found that private producers were growing radishes under plastic sheeting so that they would ripen earlier. He asked the State farm authorities why they did not do likewise and was told it would not pay. If official prices were higher, State and collective farms might show as much initiative as the owners of private plots. However, this is a matter of top policy: the price of farm products sold to consumers by State shops is absurdly and uneconomically low, as is the procurement price paid to the collective farms. As a result, the latter concentrate on fulfilling the State Plan in terms of quantity and pay little attention to quality. The State trading organizations are similarly unable to make a profit and fob the customer off with vegetables of poor quality, often actually spoiled. The trading and procurement organizations cannot hire sufficient labor to sort out the good vegetables from the rotting ones. Town workers and even members of research institutes are sent off to the storehouses to perform this unskilled task on a "voluntary" basis, at a rate of pay equal to what they receive at their regular place of employment. This, of course, inflates the cost of vegetables to the State even farther; but the authorities cannot bring themselves to increase retail and procurement prices. The average citizen's budget is pretty tight as it is, and higher prices for mass-consumption goods would have a sharp impact on public morale and, no doubt, on standards of nourishment. Compared to these dangers, the present shortage of vegetables is a lesser evil.

We have seen how efficient speculators are in market analysis and delivering fruit and vegetables from southern to northern areas. Let us now see how efficiently State organizations perform the same task. Another article in *Izvestia* in May 1973 told the following tale:[31]

> Deliveries of radishes and spring onions are not expected at Novosibirsk, Kemerovo, or Novokuznetsk, although the distributors have been allocated money and assigned their own representatives in Tashkent to procure them. *Izvestia* conducted a telephone interview on a special linkup, with the following result:
>
> *Novokuznetsk*: We've been waiting for radishes from Tashkent since May 4. The collective farms there say the stuff's all ready, we've only to collect it, but the railroad can't provide a refrigerator train. Is that so?
>
> *Tashkent railroad station*: No, it isn't. There are plenty of trains. What you need is a delivery team from Tsentrosoyuz (the Central Association of Consumers' Societies).
>
> *Tsentrosoyuz*: No, that's not the problem. Transport regulations say that radishes mustn't travel more than

three days, and it takes seven days to get to Kemerovo and Novokuznetsk. Article 78 says you can make exceptions in special cases, and we were willing, but the Ministry of Transport wasn't.

Ministry of Transport: Yes, we were, Article 78's in order.

Izvestia: So what's the problem? Leontyev of the Ministry of Transport says the radishes can be delivered promptly, and Ivanov of Tsentrosoyuz says they can be unloaded.

Deputy Minister of Trade of the RSFSR (another Ivanov): It's we who object. The radishes might be unsalable. And anyway, transport regulations say . . .

The article reporting this interesting discussion is entitled "A Special Case . . . of Radishes." There is, however, plenty of evidence that such cases are not exceptional and apply to other goods as well. In addition to the low prices, a main source of trouble is the cumbersome and inflexible regulations and the reluctance on everybody's part to take even the slightest risk.

Setting aside questions of economics and law, the essential difference between private and State producers can be summed up by saying that the former *care* about their goods. A bunch of green vegetables on a market stall is washed, neatly tied, and a pleasure to look at. In a State shop it is a repellent spectacle of withered leaves, dried mud, and roots.*

The attention to detail is especially important in the pro-

---

* Even in the republics of Central Asia, where the population consumes far more green vegetables than in European Russia and Siberia, State procurement and sale is no more efficient. To quote an Uzbek journalist writing in the newspaper *Pravda Vostoka* in 1960:[32] "Inogam Usmanov of Tashkent, a former policeman, is now a well-known shopkeeper selling greens, shredded carrots, and pastries. Why? Because there is not a single State trading organization that knows how to shred carrots or tie up a bunch of dill and parsley."

cessing of vegetables. Another article in *Izvestia* described the difference between privately sold pickles and those in government shops:[33]

> If you want nice, crisp pickles, flavored with dill and garlic and wrapped neatly in a red currant leaf, the place to go is Auntie Frosya's stall in the town market, second row on the right as you come in from the main entrance. Two rubles for a kilogram and a bit of overweight. And have you tried her juicy pickled cabbage with bilberries?—no fancy foreign names, but first-class. It costs half a ruble.
>
> "Isn't that a bit expensive?" said someone. I asked Auntie Frosya. She smiled and replied kindly in her singsong voice: "You can get them cheaper, dear, at the State store across the street. And you don't even have to stand in line there." But I didn't go to the State store. I had tried it already.

The same reporter continues:

> You and I are able to live more comfortably nowadays, we are getting better off and can afford something nice to eat. Auntie Frosya knows this and adapts her commercial activity to a steadily growing demand. But her opposite number, Antonina Vasilyevna Novikova, chief technologist of the Public Catering Trust, is not allowed to deviate from the methods and recipes for processing fruit and vegetables prescribed by the Nutritional Research Institute of the Ministry of Trade of the USSR and dating back to the postwar days when there was a shortage of cabbages, not to mention herbs and spices. Salt the cucumbers and ram them into barrels—that is all the technology amounts to. Seven pounds of garlic to a ton of cucumber—what sort of aroma or flavor can you get from that? As for cinnamon, cloves, peppercorns—all these are no longer exotic delicacies, but the rules don't say anything about them, and that's the end of it.

I do not wish to give too gloomy an impression of the fruit-and-vegetable situation in the USSR. I agree with the reporter who said that things are getting better, but demand is well ahead of supply in the official sector, and speculators seem to take full advantage of this in spite of the risks involved.

Speculation applies not only to goods that are in short supply because of the deficiencies of State planning and distribution, but to all cases in which a customer is prevented by some regulation from getting what he wants. Other countries have laws restricting speculation, but the USSR's definition of this crime is exceptionally extensive. Many countries regulate the sale of narcotics and liquor,* but in the Soviet Union there are more items prohibited for trade than elsewhere. This applies especially to the sale of foreign goods; the notion of smuggling is very broadly interpreted.

The following regulation was adopted in the RSFSR in 1963:

> It is a criminal offense to purchase bread, flour, groats, or other cereals from State or cooperative stores for the purpose of feeding livestock and poultry, or to feed them with cereals purchased. The offense is punishable by a fine under administrative regulations, or, if practiced systematically or on a large scale, by up to a year's corrective labor or imprisonment for between one and three years with or without confiscation of livestock (Article 154(1) of the Criminal Code of the RSFSR).

---

* In Russia, speculation in liquor takes the form of enabling customers to buy it during hours when liquor stores are officially closed. A writer in *Izvestia*,[34] after describing various infringements of the law governing the sale of spirits, remarks that "not all those engaged in the liquor trade are honest and high-principled." There is a special article in the Criminal Code concerning the sale of *samogon*, or home brew.

This remarkable regulation speaks for itself, but here is a case from the *Bulletin of the Supreme Court of the RSFSR* for 1974:

> Citizeness Smolyanova was convicted under Article 154(1) of the Criminal Code of the RSFSR and was sentenced, in accordance with Article 43, to a fine of 100 rubles and confiscation of her livestock, a cow and a bull calf.
>
> The sentence was imposed by the people's court of Rasskazov in the Tambov region and was upheld by the regional Judicial Collegium for Criminal Affairs.
>
> The Judicial Collegium for Criminal Affairs of the Supreme Court of the RSFSR took cognizance of the case on July 16, 1973, in light of the protest of the chairman of the Supreme Court that the sentence should not include confiscation of livestock. It upheld the appeal and ruled as follows.
>
> Smolyanova was found guilty of having, in 1971–72, systematically bought bread from Shop No. 37 and used it as fodder for her own livestock, consisting of a cow and a bull calf. On October 13, 1972, there were found in her house sixteen loaves and five and a half pounds of bread soaked in water.
>
> Smolyanova confessed her guilt in court and was convicted on the material evidence. Her offense was correctly defined and the sentence imposed was appropriate to her acts and her personal character.
>
> However, the Judicial Collegium of the Supreme Court of the RSFSR, taking into account Smolyanova's advanced age, the fact that she has been engaged in productive work for over thirty years and has no relatives to afford her material assistance, deems it possible to waive the confiscation of the cow, while confirming the sentence in other respects.

According to the 1971 *Commentary*,[35] Article 154(1) does not apply to cereals acquired elsewhere than in State and cooperative shops, nor to grain which has not been converted into groats or flour; it does, however, apply to pastry, crackers, etc.

Soviet juridical literature does not explain why the Russian people, who have been engaged in animal husbandry for centuries, should suddenly have to buy cereals and pastry from shops to feed to cattle, hogs, or poultry. Presumably, they would not do so if they could obtain proper fodder, but there is a serious dearth of this in many parts of the country, and they therefore have to break the law to feed their privately owned livestock.

According to *The Chronicle of the Lithuanian Catholic Church*, No. 16, when the authorities were anxious to dissuade the mother of Simas Kudirka from visiting her relatives in New York, representatives of the local Executive Committee and of the KGB attempted to bribe her with the promise of a meeting with her son and of hay for her cow.*

* Simas Kudirka took refuge on board an American Coast Guard cutter in 1970 and applied for political asylum. The United States authorities permitted Soviet sailors to board the American ship and remove Kudirka by force. He was sentenced to ten years' imprisonment for treason. In 1974 Kudirka was recognized to be a United States citizen (his mother had been born in Brooklyn). The Soviet government pardoned Kudirka in August 1974, after which he emigrated to the United States with his mother, wife, and children.

10

Theft of Socialist Property

As I have pointed out, the traditional Russian disrespect for State property rights has persisted into the Soviet era and has taken on greater importance since practically everything is now the property of the State. According to Article 6 of the Constitution, "The earth and its resources, waters, forests, plants, factories, mines, means of transport by rail, water and air, banks, communications, large agricultural enterprises organized by the State (State farms, machine and tractor stations, etc.), municipal undertakings and basic living accommodations in cities and industrial centers are the property of the State, that is to say of the whole people."

Assets of any consequence that are not State property fall into the category of public property, e.g., that belonging to collective farms and cooperatives. The distinction between State and public property is not reflected in the attitude of those who pilfer both indifferently, or in the law that imposes penalties for such thefts. The law does, however, take a different attitude toward the protection of socialist property (State or public) on the one hand and that of private property on the other: penalties in the former case are much more severe. It is not clear whether this is to be taken as an invitation along the lines of "If you must steal, let it be from individuals and not the State," or whether it reflects the principle that one who steals public property is a greater social danger than one who robs only private citizens.* At all events, the discrimination seems to be taken for granted, and I know of no attempt in Soviet juridical literature to justify it as opposed to simply stating it. This matter is worth serious attention, however, since the death penalty can be inflicted for large-scale theft of socialist property.

In bourgeois countries the involvement of the state's interests is not always a major factor in determining the penalty for crime, and this fact has been the subject of many doctrinaire reflections by Soviet jurists. B. S. Nikiforov, editor of the translation of Courtney S. Kenny's *Outlines of Criminal Law*,[1] commenting on the fact that in English law the penalty may be the same for bribing an official or the representative of a private concern, observes: "All these rules for the protection of the entrepreneur against dishonesty on the part of his employees are typical of bourgeois

---

* The Criminal Code speaks of crimes against the private property of *citizens*. Presumably this means Soviet citizens as opposed to foreign nationals or stateless persons. However, this is not certain, and it may be that the property of foreign nationals in the Soviet Union is also protected by law; but on the face of it, there is no protection for the property of stateless persons.

According to *Basic Principles of Civil Legislation of the USSR and Union Republics*, p. 123, "Stateless persons (literally 'persons without citizenship') living in the USSR enjoy the same rights under the law as Soviet citizens. Particular exceptions may be made by the law of the USSR." Stateless persons in the USSR "may, in accordance with the law, possess private property," and they are, therefore, by implication entitled to expect the authorities to protect their property. Stateless persons not living in the USSR, unlike foreign citizens, have no legally recognized right to hold property in the USSR.

It is hard to say how important it is in practice that crimes against the property of stateless persons are not legally punishable in the USSR. I doubt whether thieves, or even Soviet jurists, are aware of this legal loophole.

jurisprudence in the imperialist period, which sanctions the identification of the interests of individual capitalists with those of the bourgeois State."

The Soviet public also distinguishes, but in the opposite way, between stealing socialist and private property. The theft of private property is regarded by all except actual thieves as criminal and shameful, whereas the average citizen regards the theft of public property, unless it is on a large scale, as innocent and normal behavior. As a rule he does not bother to rationalize this attitude, but if he does he will say things like: "The State won't miss a trifle like that"; "If I could get it in the stores, I wouldn't steal it at work"; or "There are lots of things the State fails to provide, so we have to take them for ourselves."

A factory worker replied to a questionnaire about the theft of socialist property:* "People think it's silly to buy a thing in the shops if you can take it or make it at the place where you work. They lay hands on everything, from stationery to the most expensive fittings, which they simply rip out of their mountings." Another replied: "You may see an honest(?)† comrade, with no material worries, hunting around for a length of electric cord or a socket, a switch, a screw or a bolt, a rubber washer or a plug—anything, small or big. Some of them filch things on the sly, on a small scale, but others bring cans and demijohns and fill them up."

The same report quotes the reply of a woman in the accounting office who was convicted of pilfering and who, asked whether she regarded herself as morally on a par with burglars and pickpockets, answered: "What do you take me for—a common thief? I'd never dream of picking a pocket or taking anything from somebody's home."

---

* *The Prevention of Theft of State and Public Property* (Moscow, 1971).

† It is not clear whether the question mark in parentheses was added by the factory worker or by the jurist quoting his reply.

As is well known, the public attitude toward social phenomena is often reflected in language. The indulgence felt by the average citizen toward petty theft of public property has led to the half-affectionate term *nesun* (scrounger), meaning literally one who "lifts" or "carries off." The indulgence, of course, is strictly unofficial: at workers' meetings indignant speeches are made about *nesuny*, and a journalist has stated in *Izvestia* (January 24, 1974) that "the nesun philosophy has long been condemned by public opinion."

Condemnatory meetings, however, are not sufficient to cope with the problem of nesuny: they are subjected to disciplinary measures and made to stand trial before comrades' courts. If a person is known to be pilfering systematically, the public prosecutor's office must be informed. But managers are loath to combat pilfering too zealously because they are responsible, as ideologists frequently insist, not only for the quality and quantity of their firm's output but also for the morality of the employees. Every publicized case of the theft of socialist property is evidence of defective moral education in the enterprise concerned and is frowned on by high authority, especially Party authority. Consequently, in minor cases at least, managers prefer to wash their dirty linen at home and to hush up thefts for fear of being held indirectly responsible. Thus the system of mutual cover-up obtains, not only among workers other than activists or Party militants but also between managers and their staffs.

The authorities are aware of this, and in 1974, for instance, it was reported in *Socialist Industry* (August 24) that a special commission to combat pilfering had been set up at the *Zarya* confectionery works with a full-time secretary, presumably one specially detailed and not responsible to the works management.

For a long time many enterprises have been guarded by special security units from the Ministry of Internal Affairs.

These units are not responsible to the management, and their main function, apart from keeping out spies and saboteurs, is to prevent the theft of socialist property. As workers leave the plant, they are expected to pass through an inspection room where a guard examines their briefcases and handbags. This, in theory, is a voluntary system; it is not known who prescribes it or what the regulations are, but—except in top-secret establishments or where the guards are overzealous—regard is paid to the provision of the Constitution that guarantees personal inviolability. If workers refuse to show the contents of their bags, the guards are not supposed to open them; but if they are suspicious they can call the police, who will conduct a search despite the lack of a warrant, Constitution or no Constitution. In practice, few people, whether scientists or manual workers, refuse to submit to "voluntary" search.

Another function of the guards is to prevent workers from bringing vodka into the factory. Since they carry it in their pockets, it can be difficult to detect, especially under winter clothing. Therefore the guards run their hands over the workers' clothes, and very few complain of this indignity. However, *Izvestia* in 1974 reported a case[2] in which a worker, Boris Turanov, quit his job at a tire factory in protest against being frisked. He explained: "I was stopped in the inspection room on the way to work, but I wouldn't let them frisk me, as the law says that people who have done nothing illegal are personally immune. . . . I didn't want to leave the job, I was comfortable in the hostel there, but I didn't like the inspection system." *Izvestia* reporter G. Komrakov commented: "Turanov knows that dishonest people sometimes try to smuggle out small objects—a flashlight, a can of paint, a coil of wire—and that if you multiply this by the number involved it means a substantial loss to the State. He knows too that workers leaving the plant are required to show the contents of bags or parcels, and that when a shift goes off duty the guards are entitled to make at least a token check of their clothing if they suspect anything wrong. Turanov knows all this and accepts it, but he doesn't see why he should have to be searched on his arrival in the morning."

Komrakov quoted the deputy chief of security as saying: "If a man's overcoat is bulging, we are allowed to feel and see what's there. If it's vodka, the law says we have to take it from him and pour it out. That's what the law says." To which Komrakov commented: "The deputy chief was indulging his imagination a bit; there is no such law. Doubtless the guards act with the best intentions, but the only authority they have is an order by the manager that people found with spirits when they come on duty must be stopped and the liquor destroyed."

At all events Turanov, while sensitive on the point of personal immunity, had no objection to being searched when leaving his place of work, realizing how important this practice was in the public interest. Attempts to search customers in self-service stores have met with more resistance. Apparently the staff in many stores requested customers either to leave their bags and cases on the way in, or to let them be searched on the way out, but they took no responsibility for the safety of bags left with them. As reported by *Izvestia* (July 27, 1973), when a student complained that her briefcase full of papers had been lost by a store, she was simply told that she wasn't the first and wouldn't be the last to whom it happened.

Whether because of public protests or the constant improvement of the regulations governing Soviet life, the Ministry of Trade on May 18, 1973, issued an order forbidding sales personnel to search customers' bags, briefcases, etc.[3] While the authorities are no less thorough in their attempts to prevent shoplifting from self-service stores than in combating pilferage in factories, I believe that the former offense is less frequent, being regarded by the average citizen as theft in the full sense of the term.

Apart from pilferers, who are dealt with by fines, factory discipline, or pressure from social organizations, there is the problem of large-scale theft of socialist property. The amount of attention this crime receives in the Soviet press, which is usually reticent in reporting criminal cases, indicates that this is a frequent offense. From the figures published in 1968[4] it appears that 15 to 18 percent of all convictions in 1967 were for crimes against socialist property, while crimes against private property accounted for 16 percent of convictions.

It is impossible to enumerate even the most common varieties of the theft of socialist property. A Soviet author[5] says that: "Large-scale thefts are generally committed by organized groups including managers, accountants, and others with responsibility for handling valuable equipment, materials and money." The penalty for large-scale theft or embezzlement consists of eight to fifteen years' imprisonment with confiscation of property, or—in especially grave cases—death with confiscation of property. In Soviet practice a theft of ten thousand rubles (roughly $15,000) or more is regarded as especially grave, but the amount of the theft is not the only criterion; jurists and courts also consider the scale of the operation and nature of the State property involved.[6]

Unfortunately, juridical literature and the press rarely publish details of especially grave thefts of socialist property, but from such facts as do appear it would seem that criminals sometimes get away with large sums. Thieves who stole over a long period from a knitwear factory in the Kirgiz republic made away with State property to the value of over three million rubles; and between 1950 and 1960, a gang headed by one Goldman stole from a single plant textiles valued by the Supreme Court at 2,952,472 rubles.[7]

Theft on this scale is uncommon, but one quite often hears of thefts involving thousands or tens of thousands of rubles.

Large-scale theft of public property requires considerable business experience as well as conspiratorial ingenuity. A study of two hundred especially serious cases[8] showed that 14 percent of the frauds were carried on over a period of more than five years, 66 percent for over two years and 90 percent for over one year—figures that testify to the skill of the operators as well as the inadequacy of supervision and prevention.

In minor cases, the technique is less elaborate, and sometimes it is downright primitive. In Moscow in the late 1950s, a bus driver used a special gadget to fish money out of the coin box. He was detected by the fact that the receipts of other drivers on his route were always larger.

While thieves' methods are sometimes remarkably simple, employers use very little care in selecting their staff. A certain lady made a practice of working as a shop cashier, robbing the till and disappearing to another town, where she would repeat the process. Each time she was engaged she presented a false passport with a fake stamp and a personal details sheet bearing a number different from the number on the main document.[9]

A typical feature of Soviet life is that people often steal socialist property not for personal use but as a means of carrying on their lawful occupations. This applies especially to those who cannot get hold of raw materials and spare parts for their work. Tractor drivers and mechanics steal spare parts from one another; laboratory assistants steal one another's materials, instruments, and equipment. In many cases they do so not because of any immediate need but to be sure of having items on hand for later use. Supervisors discourage their staffs from stealing from each other, but they rarely complain if the theft is at the expense of another workshop or laboratory. Thefts of this kind seldom lead to prosecution, though no doubt an article of the Criminal Code could be found to cover them. If the person responsible is an official, he may be found guilty of theft of State property through misuse of his official position (Article 92 of the Criminal Code) as the following case illustrates.

V. I. Samarsky, a senior engineer in the neurosurgical laboratory of Leningrad's Institute of Experimental Medicine, was found to have abused his position over a two-year period by removing electronic spare parts and other equipment from the laboratory and concealing them at his home. There were 1,129 stolen articles of 57 different kinds, valued altogether at 984 rubles and 43 kopecks. On September 22, 1967, the People's Court of the Petrograd district sentenced Samarsky to three years' imprisonment under Article 92 of the Criminal Code of the RSFSR, for misusing his position in order to steal socialist property.

However, the Judicial Collegium for Criminal Affairs of the Leningrad City Court, to which the case was appealed, took note that Samarsky was responsible in the Institute's five-year plan for an important research project for influencing the nervous system by diverting and stimulating the impulses of the neurons in the brain. Fearing that the necessary equipment would not be available when the time came to start work on the project because of the scarcity of parts and their inefficient allocation, he decided to hoard the equipment at home. Two years later, after having made no use of the equipment for personal gain, he confessed his crime. The Collegium decided on November 1, 1967, that Samarsky had not acted from any mercenary motive, and that his offense fell under Article 170 of the Code, which deals simply with the misuse of authority or official position.

11
Criminal Statistics: A Detective Story

On February 11, 1968, *Pravda* informed its readers that, according to the Federal Bureau of Investigation, 3,700,000 major crimes were committed in the United States in 1967. Soviet readers apparently found this hard to believe, and so did Soviet jurists. The article continued: "Allowing for official 'cooking' of the figures, experts assume that not less than 10 million crimes are committed annually in the USA."*

From time to time Soviet readers are told how many crimes are committed in other countries, but it is a long while since they were given figures about their own crime rate. They are informed that crime in the USSR "is steadily diminishing and is many times less frequent than in pre-Revolutionary Russia."[1] At the height of Stalin's purges in the 1930s, when especially bold claims were made, the annual number of convictions was reported to be decreasing. One author stated, for example,[2] that in 1936 the total of recorded crimes in the USSR was little more than half the figure for 1934.† In the RSFSR, the total for the first six

---

* There is no precise indication of how the figure of 10 million is arrived at, or what the "falsification coefficient" applied to statistics in this and other cases might be.

† Replevsky in *Socialist Legality* (1937), No. 11.

months of 1936 was only slightly more than half the figure for the first six months of 1933, and in Byelorussia the number of convictions for the first six months of 1936 was only one quarter of the number for the first six months of 1933.

In more recent years crime has not decreased at such a rate: between 1946 and 1966, we are told, convictions decreased by 1 or 2 percent per annum on an average.[3] No absolute figures have been issued but we are told that before 1958 the number of convictions included many cases that would now be dealt with by the Comrades' Court: "Cases of brawling, slander and insult accounted for 14–16 percent of the convictions; petty theft of socialist property for 8–10 percent and petty hooliganism for 18–20 percent. Thus almost half of all the crimes were of a minor character. Before the introduction of the new Criminal Codes in 1959–61, from 30 to 40 percent of the criminal cases dealt with by People's Courts were private complaints of slander, insult and assault." From other sources we know that many cases of minor hooliganism and petty theft of socialist property are nowadays dealt with by administrative procedure, so that these, too, do not figure in conviction statistics. This being so, it is quite possible that crime actually increased during the 1946–1966 period.

Since criminal statistics were published in Russia up to 1928, we could form some idea of the present situation if Soviet authors gave figures based on a comparison with the 1920s, but such comparisons are hard to find. Kuznetsova tells us that "the rate of convictions in 1963–65 was the lowest for thirty years" (she does not say whether this means since 1933, 1934, or 1935). We can estimate the number of convictions in the RSFSR in 1933 and 1934, as Shlyapochnikov* gives figures for these years in relation to

---

* Shlyapochnikov in *Problems of Criminal Policy* (1935), Vol. 1.

the figures for 1928, and the 1928 figures are given by Kuznetsova in absolute terms.[4] Apparently the total was 955,629 convictions in 1928 and somewhat over a million in 1934. The statement quoted above can thus be taken to mean that convictions in 1963–65 were in the region of a million annually: if they were much lower than the 1934 figures, Kuznetsova would no doubt have said so.

It does not seem likely that convictions decreased much between 1963–65 and 1967; yet Ostroumov[5] tells us that the number of convictions per capita in 1967 was less than a third of what it was in 1928. This would mean, on the basis of Kuznetsova's 1928 figures, that in 1967 there were less than 317 convictions per 100,000 people. Assuming the population of the USSR in 1967 to be about 200 million, this gives a figure of 634,000 convictions in 1967, which is only two-thirds the annual figure estimated above for 1963–65—all of which shows the difficulty of arriving at consistent results on the basis of Soviet comparisons between the 1920s and 1930s and the postwar period.

Another method is to try to establish the number of crimes committed in a city or large enterprise in proportion to its population or its number of employees. Such data seldom appear in the press, but Gertsenzon in his *Introduction to Soviet Criminology* says that in the two years 1960–61, 18 crimes and 183 misdemeanors were committed in a factory with a work force of 1,300. If we assume for the sake of argument that the rate of criminality in this factory is typical of the USSR, we get a rough figure of 700 crimes per 100,000 of the population; this means 1,400,-000 crimes for a population of 200 million, or 1,750,000 for the present population of 250 million (not counting the far greater number of misdemeanors). However, there is a good deal of evidence to show that the crime rate is higher among workers, and the estimate, rough as it is, is no doubt excessive.

The Uzbek newspaper *Pravda Vostoka* stated in 1960[6] that in less than six months 3,581 people had been arrested in the secondhand market for various criminal offenses. Counting these crimes alone, we arrive at a ratio of 700 crimes per 100,000 inhabitants of Tashkent, and if the rate of criminality were uniform throughout the USSR* this would give a total of 1,750,000 crimes a year. It is interesting, although probably accidental, that this figure coincides with the figure arrived at in the previous paragraph.

All these calculations are, of course, far too imprecise to give any accurate estimate of the crime rate and number of convictions in the USSR. The most they do is to illustrate the kind of devices one has to use to guess at the facts. This is a curious state of affairs, since we are not dealing, after all, with military secrets but with sociological facts which, according to modern theory, it is every citizen's right and duty to know.

A more exact idea of the number of convictions may, I believe, be deduced from Sakharov's figure† for the present Soviet prison population—1,700,000. Taking this in conjunction with Kuznetsova's statement that 45–50 percent of the sentences imposed do not involve terms of imprisonment, and with data from which the average prison sentence can be calculated, we might deduce the number of those convicted annually in the USSR. From the information given by Sakharov about various sentences (and from Anashkin's statement that about 1 percent of all sentences are for more than 10 years),[8] I infer that the average prison sentence is 3.4 years. (A comparable figure, 4.35

---

* According to Kuznetsova,[7] the rate of criminality "as a whole, and for most of the commonest crimes" is higher for the RSFSR than for the USSR.

† Andrei Sakharov, *Sakharov Speaks* (New York, 1974), p. 45. I myself suspect that Sakharov's figure may be an understatement, but the English historian Peter Reddaway has arrived at a somewhat smaller figure, based on his estimate of the number of Soviet labor camps.

years, can be arrived at from data on prison sentences in the Moldavian republic.)* If the prison population is 1,700,000 and the average sentence is 3.4 years, this gives an average of 500,000 prison sentences a year, or a total of a million convictions, assuming half the convictions do not result in imprisonment.

The actual annual number of convictions is probably rather more than a million, since the average length of incarceration was calculated from data concerning judicial sentences. According to Anashkin,[9] not all those who are given sentences of eight to nine years serve the full term: taking into account parole and remission, over half serve only four or five years.

But accepting a rough figure of one million convictions a year, we can use the selective data given in *Sovetskaya Kriminologiya*[10] to estimate the frequency of various crimes. The results are: 200–250,000 convictions for theft of socialist property, 150–200,000 for hooliganism, 100–120,000 for crimes against the person (murder, rape, grievous bodily harm, etc.), 100–150,000 for crimes against private property and 40–50,000 for automobile offenses.

These estimates of the number of convictions do not, of course, indicate how many crimes are actually committed. We may suppose that in the case of murder and other serious crimes the detection rate is fairly high, but it is probably low in the case of hooliganism or crimes against public or private property. Soviet authors claim that over 90 percent of all crimes are solved but they do not tell us what interval elapses between a crime and the arrest of the perpetrator. If, say, the interval is five years, then in many cases the offender will have committed several more crimes during that period.

Many crimes go unrecorded either because the local

* *Problems of Crime*, No. 10. (Moscow, 1969). Moldavia, a Soviet republic that borders on Romania, was formerly known as Bessarabia.

authorities do not learn of them or because they wish to claim credit with their superiors for success in the fight against crime and therefore do not prosecute even when they have the evidence. Soviet jurists have often drawn attention to this. The criminologist I. I. Karpets, for example, observes*[11] that while vigorous action is taken, and seen to be taken, against major crimes, the same cannot be said of cases that do not constitute a serious social danger. This, he says, may be traced to various causes: the authorities have too many urgent cases, they underrate trifling ones, or they deliberately neglect their duty to give the impression that they are stabilizing or reducing the crime rate.

The journalist Arkadi Vaksberg,[12] reporting a case in which the police for a long time refrained from prosecuting a youth who committed repeated acts of assault and hooliganism, wrote:

> There may be explanations for this, and I will suggest one. We have all encountered the phenomenon of "percentage mania," which is pernicious in every field but doubly so in this. Percentages are valuable and necessary in statistics, where the purpose is to give an exact record, but they are the opposite when they are used to embellish facts. This practice was condemned some years ago by the Procurator-General of the USSR, who instructed his department to take steps ruthlessly to uncover instances of keeping crime off the record, either by not reporting it or by failing to register prosecutions. The problem is clearly a serious one; the fight against falsification goes on, but one still runs across cases of "embellishment" from time to time.

As we saw earlier, Soviet experts suspect American official figures of being "cooked," and Vaksberg is not alone in believing the same of Soviet figures. The only difference is

* I. I. Karpets, *Punishment: Social, Legal, and Criminological Problems* (Moscow, 1973).

that the Soviet experts were able, by applying a falsification coefficient, to extract information from the American data, whereas the coefficient for Soviet statistics is probably unknown even to the Soviet authorities themselves; in any case it would not help the researcher to know it, because even the cooked figures are not published.

Soviet writers, expatiating on the amount of crime in the West, make much of the number of second offenders; according to *Problems of Crime* (1969), No. 9, 70 percent of those convicted in the United States in 1966 were recidivists. This does not seem to me discreditable; on the contrary, a low proportion of recidivists suggests that crime is not confined to a particular social group but is widespread throughout the population. This, in my opinion, is the conclusion to be drawn from the fact that the proportion of second or subsequent offenders among those convicted in the USSR ranges from 25 to 33 percent.[13]

12

Prospects for the Future

According to Communist doctrine, when Communism some day becomes a reality there will, in principle, be no more crime. As Lenin put it, "We know that the fundamental social cause of violations of the rules of society is the exploitation of the masses, their want and their poverty. With the removal of this chief cause, excesses will inevitably begin to 'wither away.' We do not know how quickly and in what order, but we do know they will wither away."[1]

Soviet criminologists still profess this doctrine, though perhaps less extravagantly than in the 1930s. While Soviet doctrine asserts that the masses have been redeemed from penury and are no longer exploited, Soviet writers admit that there are still causes of crime in the USSR. In the 1930s the authorities denied that this was so as far as offenses under ordinary law were concerned, and a virtual stop was put to criminological studies. This, as Gertsenzon observes[2] in his 1965 *Introduction to Soviet Criminology*, had a deleterious effect on the work of police, prosecutors, courts, and corrective labor institutions. By the late 1950s, well after Stalin's death, jurists were again allowed to study criminology and crime prevention in the light of such statistics as were published, and even to study criminals from a sociological point of view, analyzing their personalities and the motives for their crimes.

Not many works were published as a result, but those that exist are interesting and worth further study. The opinions expressed and conclusions reached do not differ greatly from one to the next. In general, the investigators distinguish three groups of factors. The first is concerned with the criminal's personality—his psychological traits, upbringing, attitude toward work, material standard of life, and so forth. The second relates to the social environment of the criminal at the time of the crime. The third is concerned with society as a whole and what are called survivals of capitalism (or feudalism or the past).

Study of the first group of factors enables those practically concerned to reform individual criminals and to improve the education of youth in general. Study of the second enables them to tackle those institutions or sections of the community that are most infected by crime. According to Karpets, for instance,[3] a study of crime statistics in the city of Kharkov showed that the majority of offenses were committed by manual and other workers employed in 16 out of 300 enterprises. He went on to say that the collected data enabled local Party and social organizations to set about removing the causes of crime in those 16 enterprises. At the Lemash plant, which manufactures forestry machinery, these causes included:

(a) The alienation of some workers from group activities.
(b) The low level of collective educational work.
(c) Inadequate efforts to interest manual and other workers in technical training.
(d) Lack of attention to organizing recreation for the workers, especially those in hostels.
(e) A permissive attitude toward violations of the law.

As far as the third group goes, V. S. Orlov[4] states that the "survivals" include all phenomena "contrary to socialism but rooted in the ideology and morality of presocialist economic and social groups and, in particular, of present-day capitalism, the pernicious influence of which gives rise to alien views and ideas within our socialist society."

This author, like many others, includes in his long list of survivals the following vices: lack of interest in politics, lack of idealism, amorality, chauvinism, nationalism, religious prejudices and superstition, opposing one's own interests to those of the community, egoism, cupidity, careerism, vanity, hypocrisy, insincerity, mendacity, toadying, servility, want of principle, conceit, arrogance, boasting, disrespect for comrades, an unrefined attitude toward women, petty bourgeois license and lack of discipline, coarseness, disrespect for law and for the rules of communal living, idleness, parasitism, self-isolation, reactionary ideas of domesticity, an irresponsible attitude toward marriage and the upbringing of children, immorality in personal and everyday relationships, avarice, and alcoholism. Soviet authors are convinced that all these are a legacy of capitalism or the result of current capitalist influence. They are further convinced that socialism cannot itself breed such vices, and that Communism will sooner or later eradicate them.

As socialism clearly cannot itself be a breeder of crime, these authors conclude that the main cause of criminality in a socialist society is the legacy of the past and the malign influence of the outside capitalist world; these two factors are frequently lumped together as survivals of capitalism. Even crimes due to inadvertence are the result of capitalism, not socialism.

> Survivals of the past are the source and foundation not only of deliberate but of unintentional crimes. For centuries the social system based on exploitation has trained human beings to think of themselves and pay

no attention to the fate and interests of others; this leads to a careless, negligent attitude toward one's own acts, a reluctance to analyze one's behavior or to exercise caution, considerateness, and forethought.[5]

All these defects will, of course, disappear with the radiant advent of Communism.

Orlov continues: "Soviet men and women will continue to have a clear idea of what is meant by 'survivals' until such time as these alien and pernicious phenomena are no longer found in our society. To abandon this concept or lose sight of its meaning prematurely would lead to difficulties in explaining certain facts."

The last phrase is significant; indeed, but for the convenient notion of survivals, it would be much harder to explain the persistence of crime in socialist society. As it is, many Soviet authors find it hard enough to do so and evidently realize that the explanation is more ideological than sociological. Ostroumov, the author of *Soviet Judicial Statistics*, observes that while survivals make crime possible, it remains to be investigated under what conditions this possibility becomes a reality, "since, as we know, the hundreds of thousands of people infected by survivals of capitalism do not all necessarily commit crimes."

Nonetheless, combating survivals of capitalism is considered in the Soviet Union to be one of the chief ways of preventing crime, and one of the principal means to this end is Communist education of the Soviet people. Communist education is a matter not only of instilling socialist morality but of doing so as forcefully as possible, by compulsion as well as persuasion and with the maximum interference in people's private lives. The tenets of socialist or Communist morality (in Soviet writings and practice it is virtually impossible to discover the difference, if any, between the two) are in many respects no different than those of other moral systems. Zagorodnikov tells us,[6] for example, that it is a grave violation of socialist morality to murder a pregnant woman. However, the rules of such morality are nowhere specifically laid down, although Soviet family law requires parents to bring up their children in conformity with the moral code of builders of Communism,[7] and although many jurists stress the importance of inculcating the spirit of socialist morality. True, certain moral ideals are listed in the 1961 Program of the Communist Party of the Soviet Union,[8] but it does not appear that the list is intended to be exhaustive.

The theme of socialist education is a broad one, and I shall mention only a few points that have been stressed by jurists in the context of crime prevention. The following report is typical of many: "A series of crimes was committed by employees of the Elektrobytpribor factory. V. M. Kudyah, a lay assistant to the public prosecutor, investigated their cause and found that educational work at the factory had been neglected and that neither the management nor social organizations reacted to the incidence of crime as they should have done."[9] Neglect of education is a frequent diagnosis in such cases, though the investigators generally make no mention of a control group. The usual remedy is to multiply the number of lectures, club activities, sports, amateur dramatics, meetings with shock workers and war heroes, and so on. At the same time, special attention is given to individuals, especially those who have lapsed from socialist morality.

How far all this education is scientifically directed is hard to judge. As a rule, those in charge of it do not seem to have had any special pedagogical or psychological training; they are administrators, Party and trade union leaders who have plenty of other work to do. Many writers complain that they approach their task in too formal and statistical a manner, although one also reads of enthusiasts who genuinely believe that their educational work is helping to prevent crime. For instance, a policeman who gave talks on legal and moral questions and also encouraged the building of a sports ground was reported as saying: "If people get to know our laws properly they will break them less, and if young men can show their strength and agility at games they won't hang about the streets and get into trouble."[10]

There is no reason to think that hopes like this are always misplaced. According to Soviet writers, ideological education also plays a useful part. The following story is told of a ten-year-old schoolboy, Lenya S., who stole a book from the Goretsky district library in Mogilev province. "The library staff found out from his teacher that he was an orphan and had been detected several times in petty theft; the local police had a dossier on him. The librarian talked to Lenya and lent him Hector Malot's book *Sans Famille*. The boy grew interested and read several books about unhappy children before the Revolution and the life of children today. After that he began to study better, his conduct at school improved, and he gave up thieving."[11]

Not all reports are so idyllic, but probably such methods are often successful. I doubt, however, that ideology is the most effective approach. Soviet citizens, both in normal life and in prison camps, have had their fill of it; it is often stereotyped and wearisome to the educators themselves. From time to time the authorities and experts call attention to the deficiencies of ideological propaganda, and many special Party orders are issued about it. One writer has commented:

> The liquidation of the consequences of the cult of personality and the debunking of State authorities caused some young people to distrust all authority. They were thus led astray as regards discipline and democratic institutions and fell into a demagogic habit of mind, tending inevitably toward slackness, disregard of official requirements, misconduct and crime. During and

immediately after the war the younger generation was
brought up on stories, novels, tales and songs about
our great civil and military leaders, but in recent years
little use has been made of all this immensely valuable
material.[12]

Ideology in the Soviet Union is not a separate branch of
education, it permeates the whole, and perhaps this is why
attempts to organize people's leisure are relatively unsuccessful; sports and group activities of all kinds become life-
less and perfunctory as they are turned into ideological
campaigns. The following slogans give an idea of the regimentation of the lives of schoolchildren in the Moskvoretsky district of Moscow in the 1960s:[13]

"Universal education!"

"Cleanliness and tidiness in our classrooms and play-
grounds!"

"For the good reputation of our street and playground!"

"More power to the Timur organization!" i.e., boy scout
activities of helping old people, soldiers' families, etc.

"Save scrap metal! Save electric power!"

While these objectives are not in themselves ideological,
the slogan-type formulation strengthens their association
with ideological propaganda.

In addition to active educational measures, care is taken
to protect the public from corruption by unsuitable information, such as works of art or films that are thought dangerous to morality. I have written elsewhere[14] of Soviet
censorship; here I will say only that in some cases it is
criticized as too liberal by both educators and the public.
Juridical literature refers more than once to the pernicious
effect of some foreign films on Soviet youth. V. S. Orlov
relates, for instance,[15] that young people arrested at Rostov for theft and other crimes declared in almost every case
that they had learned about "all that sort of thing" from
films. Asked which ones, they replied: *"The Magnificent*

Seven, The Black Mask, The Casino Affair, and *The Skin-heads."* Ordinary citizens, it appears, protest effectively against such films.[16] A letter was published in *Izvestia* entitled "No Visa for *The Black Mask,"* and following other protests the Film Committee of the Council of Ministers of the USSR announced measures to select the foreign films shown in the Soviet Union more carefully, to increase the supply of patriotic films for children and young people, and to revive films made in the 1930s and 1940s on heroic and revolutionary themes.[17]

The Soviet authorities appear to consider censorship an effective means of combating offenses against ordinary law, and crime may actually be reduced by the fact that no criminals are shown on Soviet screens. It could even be argued that if the channels of information were so sterilized that no one heard of the possibility of murder, no murders would be committed—yet the first murder (Genesis 4:8) was committed without anybody's instigation. Be that as it may, such sterilization is not practicable and would not be acceptable ideologically, since it would preclude educational references to the heroic revolutionary past.

The Soviet people are resistant to education, not least because of the atmosphere of public hypocrisy. Everyone knows quite well that speakers at meetings and lectures often lie brazenly to an audience that knows they are lying. This is considered proper, and everyone is used to it, but it does not increase the likelihood that the lecturer's good advice will be followed. Young people are perhaps more sensitive to hypocrisy than others; many are distressed by the atmosphere of lying, and in some it causes a real spiritual trauma. One young offender told the following tale:

> What corrupted me was the children's home. On our last day there, when we had packed our bags and were ready to go off to different factory jobs, the head called us into a study for what he said would be a friendly

talk. As it proceeded a girl from our class ran in and
said: 'He's fooling you. They're searching our bags in
the corridor.' We ran out, and so they were—to make
sure we hadn't stolen anything. On that day I stopped
believing in a lot of things. They're decent people on
the outside, but scoundrels on the inside.[18]

The authorities persistently remind the Soviet public that
the fight against crime is the responsibility of every citizen.
There are many complaints, in the Soviet Union as in other
countries, that people refuse to become involved on the
streets or in the subway when incidents of theft or hooliganism occur. I suspect, however, that a comparative study
would show that bystanders in Russia are more likely than
in other countries to assist the victims of crimes and to help
the authorities apprehend criminals. I do not know whether
this is due to the success of Communist education or to some
deep-rooted sociological factors.

Many private individuals take a more active role in police
and judicial activities, often through participation in such
organizations as the Comrades' Courts and the Volunteer
Auxiliary Police. The record of public groups cooperating
with the courts, the procuracy and the security organs is a
sad one in Soviet history. The chief function assigned these
groups by the authorities has been "signaling," their euphe-
mism for informing. The Worker and Peasant Correspondents, Stakhanovites (shock workers) and other activists
have been publicly praised for their "signaling" work.

Sometimes such actions are spontaneous. The authorities
encourage individuals to write denunciations, to "expose"
their colleagues and petty officials at public meetings, to
communicate their suspicians to Party organizations, and
even to investigate on their own any suspicious behavior of
their neighbors or acquaintances. The strange thing is that
the public does not especially censure such behavior.

This kind of amateur activity can seriously interfere with

the normal functioning of the police and the courts. The epidemic of denunciations during the Stalin era convinced the authorities of that, and for a time after Stalin's death, informing was not encouraged. But it is no secret that the authorities find informers useful, and that in Russia they exist in almost every institution and apartment building.

The authorities do more than simply pay attention to voluntary informers. Articles 88–1 and 190 of the RSFSR Criminal Code prescribe sentences of up to three years of imprisonment for failure to report the preparation or commission of serious crimes. Although failure to report the commission of petty crimes is not subject to criminal punishment, it is considered morally reprehensible. *Crimes Against Justice* (Moscow: Kulberg, 1962) states:

> It is the moral duty of every Soviet citizen to assist the fight against crime by every means including reporting the commission or preparation of crimes to the appropriate authorities.

And these are not just empty words. A person is likely to be reprimanded at public meetings for failure to show sufficient diligence in "signaling."

Knowingly false denunciations are punishable by law, but prosecutions on this charge are rare. History shows that even strict punishment for false denunciations will not stop this sort of "patriotic" activity. In medieval Russia, all who cried treason were subject to the test of torture. But such charges were still brought. It seems unlikely that the few current and unpublicized trials for false denunciations will deter informers. Although present officials are not so frank, a speaker at a Party conference in the 1920s proposed the elimination of criminal responsibility for false accusations:

> You know how timid the average Russian is. You know that it is impossible to fight the sharply rising crime rate until every citizen realizes that making an

accusation in court is not dishonorable; it is his duty. If you want to encourage such actions, if you want to instill confidence, then make informing easier and don't frighten people with responsibility for false accusations.

The authorities burden society not just with police and judicial functions but also with the task of correction. The practice of releasing offenders to the "surety of social collectives" is not so popular now as it was in the 1960s, but it still exists. If a sentence is suspended, the offender is supposed to come under the supervision of the collective at his place of work. Petty offenders are also subject to such supervision. But perhaps the oddest responsibility assigned to society results from the provision permitting judges to sentence a defendant to "social censure." Perhaps it has not occurred to the legislature and the judges that this provision turns society into the subject of the sentence; society is assigned the task of censuring a person. This is similar to the medieval practice of sentencing criminals to church penance, thereby imposing on the religious authorities the task of correction.

In conclusion I would say that although Communist hopes for the complete eradication of crime are unlikely to be fulfilled, as far as serious crimes against ordinary law are concerned, crime in the Soviet Union is not as bad as it is in some other countries. This can be attributed to such features of Soviet society as total control over the population and the compulsory nature of labor, and to specific anti-crime measures such as the ban on carrying arms. On the other hand, some measures that play a part in the prevention of crime, like the ban on private weapons and the regulations that control a person's choice of residence, themselves give rise to violations and thus swell the catalog of minor offenses. As far as major crimes are concerned, they seem to be increasing throughout the world, and it is likely that they will increase in the Soviet Union as well.

As I have noted, legislative changes may produce a deceptive decline in crime statistics, such as occurred when a number of minor offenses were transferred to the jurisdiction of Comrades' Courts. Apart from this, the Soviet authorities could reduce their crime rate if they ceased to prosecute normal activities that harm no one, like private enterprise or speculation. There is, however, little hope of their doing so. They are more likely to make greater use of the proven method of preventive administrative action, like local police forces who use the regulations for deporting idlers to get rid of many individuals whom they regard as potential criminals.

Bibliographical Notes

Translator's Note

Additional bibliographic references for those who can read Russian-language sources are contained in the Russian-language edition of this book, *Ugolovnaya Rossiya* (New York: Khronika Press, 1977).

The complete texts of the 1960 RSFSR Criminal Code and Code of Criminal Procedure as amended to March 1, 1972, are available in *Soviet Criminal Law and Procedure*, ed., Harold Berman, 2nd ed. (Cambridge: Harvard University Press, 1972). This book also contains an excellent introduction on the history and development of Soviet criminal law.

An English translation of the 1922 Criminal Code was published as *The Penal Code of the RSFSR* (London: H. M. Stationery Office, 1925). The translation of the 1926 Code was published as *The Penal Code of the RSFSR* (London: H. M. Stationery Office, 1934).

Recent American studies of Soviet crime based largely on published Soviet sources include *Deviance in Soviet Society: Crime, Delinquency, and Alcoholism* (New York: Columbia University Press, 1972), by Walter Connor, a sociologist, and *Revolutionary Law and Order* (New York: The Free Press, 1976), by the political scientist Peter Juviler.

Books by former Soviet prisoners that contain their observations on Soviet criminals met in labor camps include Edward Kuznetsov's *Prison Diaries* (New York: Stein & Day, 1975); Anatoly Marchenko's *My Testimony* (New York: E. P. Dutton, 1969); Alexander Solzhenitsyn's *The Gulag Archipelago* (New York: Harper & Row,

Vol. 1, 1974; Vol. 2, 1975; Vol. 3 forthcoming); Abram Tertz's (Andrei Sinyavsky) *A Voice from the Chorus* (New York: Farrar, Straus & Giroux, 1976).

1 The Russian Criminal Tradition

1. S. Maximov, "Narodnye prestupleniya i neschastiya" (National Crimes and Misfortunes), in *Otechestvennye zapiski* (Fatherland Notes), Vol. 183, March–April 1869.
2. Yakushkin, *Obychnoye pravo* (Customary Law), Introduction to Vol. 1.
3. (Prince) V. V. Tenishchev, "Obshchie nachala ugolovnogo prava v ponimanii russkogo krestyanina" (General Principles of Criminal Law as Understood by the Russian Peasant) in *Zhurnal ministerstva yustitsii* (Journal of the Ministry of Justice), 1909, No. 77.
4. A. A. Levenstim, "Suyeverie v ego otnoshenii k ugolovnomu pravu" (Superstition and Criminal Law), *Journal of the Ministry of Justice*, 1897, 1, 2.
5. Tenishchev, *op. cit.*
6. *Andrei Tverdokhlebov v zashchitu prav cheloveka* (Andrei Tverdokhlebov in Defense of Human Rights). New York: Khronika Press, 1975.
7. Maximov, *op. cit.*
8. *Moskovskye vedomosti* (Moscow Gazette), 1883, No. 70. Quoted from Yakushkin, *op. cit.*, Vol. 2, No. 765.
9. Yakushkin, *op. cit.*, Vol. 2, No. 717.
10. *Ibid.*, Introduction to Vol. 1.
11. Brokgauz and Efron, *Entsiklopedichesky slovar* (Encyclopedic Dictionary), Vol. 13, p. 607.
12. *Russkiye vedomosti* (Russian Gazette), 1885, No. 14.
13. Yakushkin, *op. cit.*, Vol. 2, No. 733.
14. *Ibid.*, No. 746.
15. *Ibid.*, No. 646.
16. *Russkiye vedomosti* (Russian Gazette), 1879, No. 2, p. 2.
17. Maximov, *op. cit.*
18. Yakushkin, *op. cit.*, see note 2 above.
19. *Ibid.*, Vol. 2, No. 779.
20. *Ibid.*, No. 726.
21. *Ibid.*, No. 515.

22. Tenishchev, *op. cit.*
23. Yakushkin, *op. cit.*, Vol. 2, No. 2107.
24. Levenstim, *op. cit.*
25. T. Segalov, "P'yanye draki" (Brawls), in *Problemy prestupnost* (Problems of Crime), No. 2, Moscow-Leningrad, 1927.
26. P. A. Dubovets, *Otvetstvennost za telesnoe povrezhdenie po sovetskomu ugolovnomu pravu* (Responsibility for Physical Injury in Soviet Criminal Law), Moscow, 1964, p. 136.

2   The Soviet Criminal Tradition

1. A. Melnikov, "Kolebaniya prestupnosti" (Fluctuations of Criminality), *Journal of the Ministry of Justice*, 1917, Nos. 5–6, p. 61.
2. D. S. Likhachev, "Cherty pervobytnogo primitivizma vorovskoy rechi" (Features of the Original Primitivism of Thieves' Language), in *Yazyk i myshlenie* (Language and Thought), Vol. 3–4, Moscow-Leningrad, 1935.
3. A. Avtorkhanov, "Zarozhdenie kriminalnogo techeniya v bolshevizme [eksy]" (The Beginnings of Criminality among the Bolsheviks [the 'Exes']), in *Proiskhozhdenie partokratii* (The Origin of Party Rule), Vol. 1.
4. *Istoriya gosudarstva i prava* (History of State and Law), Part 11 Moscow, 1966, p. 67.
5. Valery Chalidze, *To Defend These Rights: Human Rights and the Soviet Union.* New York: Random House, 1975.
6. "XVI syezd VKP (b)—stenografichesky otchet" (Stenographic Record of the XVIth Congress of the All-Union Communist Party [Bolsheviks]).
7. *Ibid.*
8. Ugolovny kodeks RSFSR (Criminal Code of the RSFSR), 1922.
9. Polozhenie o voiskikh prestupleniyakh—postanovlenie TSIK i SNK SSSR ot 27 iyulya 1927 g. (The Position regarding Military Crimes—Decree by the Central Executive Committee and the Council of People's Commissars, July 27, 1927), Soviet Laws 1927, No. 50.
10. *Istorichesky vestnik* (Historical Bulletin), 1884, Vol. 4, p. 623.
11. O kvalifikatsii samosudov—postanovlenie Plenuma Verkhovnogo Suda SSSR, 23 oktyabrya 1933 g. (On the Definition of Acts of Private Revenge—Decision by the Plenum of the Supreme Court of the USSR, October 23, 1933). See *Sbornik*

deystvuyushchikh postanovleniy plenuma i direktivnykh pisem Verkhovnogo Suda SSSR. 1924–1944 (Collection of Decisions of the Plenum and Directive Letters of the Supreme Court of the USSR in force from 1924 to 1944), Moscow, 1946, p. 69.

3   The Professional Underworld

1. *Pravitelstvenny vestnik* (Government Gazette), 1878, 162.
2. Yulian Semenov, "Podopechnye leytenanta Matveyeva" (Lieutenant Matveyev's Wards), in *Literaturnaya gazeta* (Literary Gazette), June 20, 1973, p. 12.
3. V. V. Krestovsky, *Sobranie sochinenii* (Collected Works), Vol. 1, 1899.
4. Gryunvald (Grünwald), "Yuridicheskaya storona arteley" (The Juridical Aspect of Artels), in *Zhurnal grazhdanskogo i ugolovnogo prava* (Journal of Civil and Criminal Law), 1876, 2.
5. Yakushkin, *op. cit.*, Introduction to Vol. I; see note 2, chapter 1.
6. *Ibid.*, Vol. 2.
7. S. Maximov, *Otechestvennye zapiski* (Fatherland Notes), 1869, No. 182.
8. Yakushkin, *op. cit.*, Vol. 2.
9. Lev Sheinin, *Zapiski sledovatelya* (Notes of a Criminal Investigator), Moscow, 1968, p. 322.
10. Likhachev, *op. cit.*; see note 2, chapter 2.
11. Shalamov, "Zhenshchiny prestupnogo mira" (Women of the Underworld), in *Grani*, Frankfurt, 1970, No. 77.
12. Likhachev, *op. cit.*; see note 2, chapter 2.
13. *Soviet Prison Camp Speech: A Survivor's Glossary.* Supplemented by terms from the works of A. I. Solzenicyn [Solzhenitsyn]. Compiled by Meyer Galler and Harlan E. Marquess. Madison: University of Wisconsin Press, 1972.
14. Maximov, *op. cit.*; see note 7 above.
15. A. F. Koshko, *Ocherki ugolovnogo mira tsarskoy Rossii* (Sketches of the Underworld of Tsarist Russia), Paris, 1926.
16. *Literaturnaya gazeta* (Literary Gazette), April 3, 1974, p. 12.
17. Sergievsky, "Nakazanie v russkom prave XVII v." (Punishment in 17th-century Russian Law), quoted from Gernet's article in *Pravo i zhizn* (Law and Life), 1923, No. 3.
18. S. Maximov in *Vestnik Evropy* (The European Messenger), 1868, No. 4.

19. Gernet, "Ocherki tyuremnoy psikhologii" (Sketches of Prison Psychology), in *Pravo i zhizn* (Law and Life), 1923, Nos. 9–10.
20. M. N. Gernet, "Tatuirovka v mestakh zaklyucheniya g. Moskvy" (Tattooing in Moscow City Prisons). See *Prestupny mir Moskvy* (Moscow's Underworld), Moscow, 1924; p. 218.
21. M. Avdeyeva, "Tatuirovka v mestakh zaklyucheniya" (Tattooing in Prison), in *Pravo i zhizn* (Law and Life), 1927, No. 1.

5 Hooliganism

1. Bashilov, "O khuliganstve kak prestupnom yavlenii, ne predusmotrennym zakonom" (Hooliganism as a Criminal Phenomenon not Envisaged by the Law), in *Journal of the Ministry of Justice*, 1913, No. 2.
2. V. Vlasov, "Khuliganstvo v gorode i derevne" (Hooliganism in Town and Country), in *Problemy prestupnosti* (Problems of Criminality), Moscow-Leningrad, Series 2, 1927.
3. Rabochy sud (Workers' Court), 1926, No. 22, p. 1359.
4. Krylenko, "Chto takoye khuliganstvo" (What is Hooliganism?), in *ibid.*, No. 22, p. 1399.
5. N. F. Kuznetsova, *Prestuplenie i prestupnost'* (Crime and Criminality), Moscow, 1969.
6. Instruktsiya (Instruction) No. 27 of February 5, 1927. See *Sbornik tsirkulyarov Narodnogo komissariata yustitsii RSFSR, deystvuyushchikh na 1 iyunya 31 g.* (Collection of Circulars of the People's Commissariat of Justice of the RSFSR, in force on June 1, 1931.)
7. *Sobranie uzakoneniy Krymskoy avtonomnoy respubliki* (Collection of Statutes of the Crimean Autonomous Republic), 1926, No. 3.
8. *Khuliganstvo i prestuplenie* (Hooliganism and Crime), collection of articles, Moscow-Leningrad, 1927.
9. *Sovetskaya yustitsiya* (Soviet Justice), 1936, No. 1, p. 10.
10. Criminal Code of the RSFSR, *Soviet Criminal Law and Procedure*, 2nd edition, ed. Harold Berman, Cambridge: Harvard University Press, 1972.
11. Sarychev case: *Khronika tekushchikh sobitiy* (A Chronicle of Current Events), No. 8, *samizdat*, 1969.
12. Zemtsov case: *ibid.*, No. 14, *samizdat*, 1970.
13. *Nauchny kommentari sudebnoy praktiki za 1967 g.* (Analytic

Commentary on Judicial Practice in 1967), Moscow, 1968, pp. 189–95.

14. *Ibid.*
15. V. V. Shubin, *Sudebnaya praktika po delam o khuliganstve* (Court Practice in Cases of Hooliganism), in *ibid.*, p. 180.
16. *Sbornik postanovleniy Prezidiuma i opredeleniy Sudebnoy kollegii po ugolovnym delam Verkhovnogo Suda RSFSR 1964– 1972* (Collection of Decisions by the Presidium and Rulings by the Judicial Collegium for Criminal Affairs of the Supreme Court of the RSFSR, 1964–1972), Moscow, 1974.
17. A. A. Gertsenzon, *Ugolovnoye pravo i sotsiologiya* (Criminal Law and Sociology), Moscow, 1970.
18. *Collection of Decisions*; see note 16 above.
19. *Preduprezhdenie prestupnosti nesovershennoletnikh* (The Prevention of Juvenile Crime) Moscow, 1965.
20. Gromov, "Bezmotivnoye prestuplenie" (Motiveless Crime: On Hooliganism), in *Journal of the Ministry of Justice*, 1913, No. 5.
21. Bashilov, *op. cit.*, p. 222; see note 1 above.
22. *Sovetskaya yustitsiya* (Soviet Justice), 1936, No. 14, p. 3.
23. Dubovets, *op. cit.*; see note 26, chapter 1.
24. *Bulletin of the Supreme Court of the RSFSR*, 1962, No. 8.
25. Gertsenzon, *op. cit.*; see note 17 above.
26. I. G. Filanovsky, *Sotsialno-psikhologicheskoye otnoshenie sub'yekta k prestupleniyu* (The Sociopsychological Relation of the Criminal to His Crime), Leningrad, 1970.
27. *Bulletin of the Supreme Court of the RSFSR*, 1963, No. 7.
28. "Ob usilenii otvetstvennosti za melkoye khuliganstvo" (On Increasing the Penalty for Petty Hooliganism). Ruling (*Ukaz*) by the Presidium of the Supreme Court of the USSR, in *Vedomosti VS SSSR* (Gazette of the Supreme Court of the USSR), 1966, No. 30.
29. Gertsenzon, *op. cit.*; see note 17 above.
30. *Bulletin of the Supreme Court of the RSFSR*, 1963, No. 9.
31. *Hooliganism and Crime*; see note 8 above.
32. G. S. Sarkisov, *Preduprezhdenie narushenii obshchestvennogo poryadka* (The Prevention of Violations of Public Order), Yerevan, 1972.
33. A. A. Gertsenzon, *Vvedenie v sovetskuyu kriminologiyu* (Introduction to Soviet Criminology), Moscow, 1965.
34. Filanovsky, *op. cit.*; see note 26 above.
35. N. S. Tagantsev, ed., *Ulozhenie o nakazaniyakh ugolovnykh i*

ispravitel'nykh 1885 goda (Criminal and Correctional Code, 1885), 6th ed., St. Petersburg, 1912.

36. *Pravo i zhizn* (Law and Life), 1926, Nos. 8–10, p. 82.
37. Sentence on Bitszel, and Chalidze's objection: *Obshchestvennye problemy* (Social Problems), No. 9, 1971; *samizdat*.
38. Ruling of the Presidium of the Supreme Court of the RSFSR, April 7, 1960: "Ob otvetstvennosti za nezakonnoye izgotovlenie i ispolzovanie radioperedayushchikh ustroystv" (Penalties for the Illegal Manufacture and Use of Radio Transmitting Apparatus), in *Vedomosti VS RSFSR* (Gazette of the Supreme Court of the RSFSR), 1960, No. 13.
39. S. Krylov, "Sovetskoye pravo o radiosvyazi i radioveshchanii" (Soviet Law on Radio Communication and Broadcasting), in *Sotsialisticheskaya zakonnost* (Socialist Legality), 1938, No. 3, p. 77.
40. "Radiopravo" (Radio Law): see *Entsiklopediya gosudarstva i prava* (Encyclopedia of State and Law), ed. P. Stuchek, Vol. 3, p. 458.
41. Decision by the Plenum of the Supreme Court of the USSR, July 3, 1963, in *Sbornik postanovleniy Plenuma VS SSSR 1924–1970* (Collection of Decisions by the Plenum of the Supreme Court of the USSR, 1924–1970), Moscow, 1970, p. 515.

6 Murder

1. S. V. Borodin, *Rassmotrenie sudom ugolovnykh del ob ubiystvakh* (Judicial Procedure in Murder Trials), Moscow, 1964.
2. V. N. Kudryavtsev, *Prichinnost' v kriminologii* (Causality in Criminology), Moscow, 1968; p. 42.
3. S. V. Borodin, *Kvalifikatsiya ubiystva po deystvuyushchemu zakonodatelstvu* (The Definition of Murder under Existing Law), Moscow, 1964, p. 132.
4. E. F. Podbegaylo, *Umyshlennye ubiystva i borba s nimi* (Deliberate Murder and Its Prevention), Voronezh, 1965.
5. *Ibid.*, p. 131.
6. Borodin, *The Definition of Murder*, p. 112; see note 3 above.
7. *Voprosy borby s prestupnostyu, vyp. 14* (Problems of Crime Prevention, Series 14), Moscow, 1971.
8. N. I. Zagorodnikov, *Prestupleniya protiv zhizni* (Crimes against Life), Moscow, 1961.
9. Podbegaylo, *op. cit.*, p. 167; see note 4 above.

10. Borodin, *Judicial Procedure*; see note 1 above.
11. Segalov, *op. cit.*; see note 25, chapter 1.
12. Gertsenzon, *Introduction to Soviet Criminology*; see note 33, chapter 5.
13. Podbegaylo, *op. cit.*, p. 135; see note 4 above.
14. *Ibid.*, p. 103.
15. *Bulletin of the Supreme Court of the RSFSR*, 1962, No. 7.
16. Borodin, *The Definition of Murder*, p. 57; see note 3 above.
17. *Ibid.*, p. 53.
18. *Ibid.*, p. 55.
19. Filanovsky, *op. cit.*, p. 83; see note 26, chapter 5.
20. Borodin, *The Definition of Murder*, p. 60; see note 3 above. Also Zagorodnikov, *op. cit.*, p. 132; see note 8 above.
21. Borodin, *The Definition of Murder*, p. 240; see note 3 above.
22. Podbegaylo, *op. cit.*, p. 175; see note 4 above.
23. *Ibid.*, p. 175.
24. Borodin, *The Definition of Murder*, p. 66; see note 3 above.
25. Podbegaylo, *op. cit.*, p. 177; see note 4 above.
26. *Izvestia* (News), July 6, 1973, p. 4.
27. *The New York Times*, October 20, 1974, p. 6.
28. *Pravo i zhizn* (Law and Life), 1923, Nos. 7–8.
29. *Ibid.*, 1925, Nos. 4–5.
30. Borodin, *The Definition of Murder*, p. 132; see note 3 above.
31. Podbegaylo, *op. cit.*, p. 131; see note 4 above.
32. *Ibid.*
33. Zagorodnikov, *op. cit.*, p. 175; see note 8 above.
34. Borodin, *Judicial Procedure*, p. 41; see note 1 above.
35. Gertsenzon, *Introduction to Soviet Criminology*; see note 33, chapter 5.
36. *Problems of Crime Prevention*, Series 1, pp. 43 ff.; see note 7 above.
37. Vasilevsky, *Detskaya prestupnost' i detsky sud* (Child Delinquency and Children's Courts), 1923.
38. Anatoly Marchenko, *My Testimony*, New York: E. P. Dutton & Co., 1969.
39. Chalidze, *op. cit.*; see note 5, chapter 2.
40. *Journal of the Ministry of Justice*, 1864, No. 2, p. 707.
41. Yakushkin, *op. cit.*, Introduction to Vol. 1; see note 2, chapter 1.
42. *Ibid.*
43. On the Beilis case, see Morris Samuel, *Blood Accusation*, New York, 1967.

44. Krylenko, *Sudebnye rechi* (Speeches in Court), Moscow, 1964.
45. "Medvezh'ya prisyaga u ostyakov" (The Bear Oath among the Ostyaks), in *Etnograficheskoye obozrenie* (Ethnographic Review), 1898, No. 3.
46. A. F. Koni, *Sobranie sochineniy* (Collected Works), Moscow, 1964, Vol. 3, p. 474.
47. V. G. Korolenko, *Sobranie sochineniy* (Collected Works), Moscow, 1971, Vol. 6, p. 5.
48. Borodin, *Judicial Procedure*, p. 189; see note 1 above.
49. On the Dandaron case, see *A Chronicle of Current Events*, Nos. 28–31, pp. 24–28; London: Amnesty International Publications, 1975.
50. *Sovetskaya kriminologiya* (Soviet Criminology), Moscow, 1966, p. 75.
51. Borodin, *Judicial Procedure*; see note 1 above.
52. *Collection of Decisions*, p. 255; see note 16, chapter 5.
53. *Collection of Statutes of the RSFSR*, 1928, No. 141, p. 927.
54. L. D. Gaukhman, *Bor'ba s nasil'stvennymi posyagatel'stvami* (The Prevention of Violent Assault), Moscow, 1959, p. 65.
55. Borodin, *The Definition of Murder*, p. 122; see note 3 above.
56. *Bulletin of the Supreme Court of the RSFSR*, 1962, No. 6.
57. Zagorodnikov, *op. cit.*, p. 234; see note 8 above.
58. *Sbornik deystvuyushchikh raz'yasnenii VS RSFSR, izdannykh za vremya s 1923 g. do 1 yanvarya 1929 g.* (Collection of Presently Valid Explanations by the Supreme Court of the RSFSR, issued between 1923 and January 1, 1929), Moscow, 1930; p. 280.
59. Zagorodnikov, *op. cit.*, p. 126; see note 8 above.
60. *Ibid.*, p. 177.
61. *Kriminologiya* (Criminology), Moscow, 1968.
62. Zagorodnikov, *op. cit.*, pp. 162–63; see note 8 above.
63. Podbegaylo, *op. cit.*, p. 12; see note 4 above.
64. N. N. Belyavsky, *Politseyskoye pravo* (Police Law), Petrograd, 1915.
65. *Prestupleniya protiv nesovershennoletnikh* (Crimes Against Minors), ed. Ya. A. Perel' and A. A. Lyubimov, 1932.
66. "Raz'yasnenie Verkovnogo suda RSFSR po delu 1923g. No. 645" (Explanation of the Supreme Court of the RSFSR concerning Case No. 645 of 1923). See *ibid.*, p. 18.
67. *Collection of Presently Valid Explanations*, p. 286; see note 58 above.
68. Podbegaylo, *op. cit.*, p. 85; see note 4 above.

69. Borodin, *The Definition of Murder*, p. 232; see note 3 above.
70. Zagorodnikov, *op. cit.*, p. 176; see note 8 above.
71. Ulozhenie o nakazaniyakh (Penal Code).
72. *Sovetskaya yustitsiya* (Soviet Justice), 1936, No. 18.
73. *Sotsialisticheskaya zakonnost'* (Socialist Legality), 1936, No. 11, p. 20.
74. *Problems of Crime Prevention*, Series 1, p. 74; see note 7 above.
75. A. E. Natashev and N. A. Struchkov, *Osnovy teorii ispravitel'no-trudovogo prava* (Foundations of the Theory of Corrective Labor Law), Moscow, 1967, p. 175.
76. "Instruksiya po neotlozhnoy gospitalizatsii psikhicheski bol'nykh, predstavlyayushchikh obshchestvennuyu opasnost'" (Instructions on the Immediate Hospitalization of Mentally Diseased Persons Constituting a Danger to Society), 1971. Extracts in *A Chronicle of Current Events*, No. 28, London: Amnesty International Publications, 1975.
77. M. K. Aniyants, *Otvetstvennost' za prestupleniya protiv zhizni* . . . (Responsibility for Crimes against Life . . .), Moscow, 1964, p. 179.
78. *Problems of Crime Prevention*, Series 1, p. 87; see note 7 above.
79. Tenishchev, *op. cit.*, p. 141; see note 3, chapter 1.
80. Alexander Solzhenitsyn, *The Gulag Archipelago*, New York: Harper & Row, 1974–75, Vol. 2.
81. Borodin, *The Definition of Murder*, p. 150; see note 3 above.

7   Sexual Crimes

1. Gertsenzon, *Criminal Law*; see note 17, chapter 5.
2. N. Sokolov and I. Chupalenkov, *Sovetsky sud* (Soviet Courts), Moscow, 1973, p. 34.
3. B. Zmiev, "Prestupleniya v oblasti polovykh otnosheniy" (Crimes in the Field of Sexual Relations), in *Problemy prestupnosti* (Problems of Criminality), No. 2, 1927.
4. *Collection of Decisions*, p. 301; see note 16, chapter 5.
5. *Problems of Crime Prevention*, Series 2, p. 39; see note 7, chapter 6.
6. *Bulletin of the Supreme Court of the RSFSR*, 1963, No. 3.
7. *Nauchny kommentari sudebnoy praktiki za 1969 g.* (Analytic Commentary on Judicial Practice in 1969), Moscow, 1970, p. 178.

8. Gertsenzon, *Criminal Law*; see note 17, chapter 5.

9. *Kommentari k Ugolovnomu kodeksu RSFSR* (Commentary on the Criminal Code of the RSFSR), Moscow, 1971, p. 283.

10. *Bulletin of the Supreme Court of the RSFSR*, 1974, No. 2.

11. Podbegaylo, *op. cit.*, pp. 111–13; see note 4, chapter 6.

12. Borodin, *Judicial Procedure*; see note 1, chapter 6.

13. Dubovets, *op. cit.*, p. 127; see note 26, chapter 1.

14. Gertsenzon, *Criminal Law*; see note 17, chapter 5.

15. *Sbornik opredeleniy Ugolovnoy kassatsionnoy kollegii VS RSFSR* (Collection of Rulings of the Criminal Appeal Division of the Supreme Court of the RSFSR), 1925, No. 1, p. 167.

16. *Bulletin of the Supreme Court of the RSFSR*, 1974, No. 2.

17. *Ibid.*, 1963, No. 5.

18. *Collection of Presently Valid Explanations*, p. 283; see note 58, chap. 6.

19. *Vestnik sovetskoy yustitsii* (Soviet Justice Bulletin), 1928, No. 17, p. 505.

20. *Commentary on the Criminal Code*; see note 9 above.

21. Gertsenzon, *Criminal Law*; see note 17, chapter 5.

22. *Commentary on the Criminal Code*; see note 9 above.

23. *Kurs sovetskogo ugolovnogo prava* (Course of Soviet Criminal Law), Leningrad, 1973, Vol. 3, p. 656.

24. *Ibid.*

25. *Commentary on the Criminal Code*; see note 9 above.

26. *Sbornik postanovleniy Prezidiuma i opredeleniy Sudebnoy kollegii po ugolovnym delam VS RSFSR, 1957–59* (Collection of Decisions by the Presidium and Rulings by the Judicial Collegium for Criminal Affairs of the Supreme Court of the RSFSR, 1957–59), Moscow, 1960, p. 189.

27. *Course of Soviet Law*; see note 23 above.

28. Gertsenzon, *Criminal Law*; see note 17, chapter 5.

29. Valery Chalidze in the *Chicago Tribune*, 1973.

8 Bribery

1. I. P. Kucheryavy, *Otvetstvennost' za vzyatochnichestvo* (Responsibility for Bribery), Moscow, 1957.

2. *O vzyatochnichestve* (On Bribery), Decree of the Council of People's Commissars of the RSFSR, *Collection of Statutes of the RSFSR*, 1918, No. 35, p. 467.

3. Kucheryavy, *op. cit.*; see note 1 above.
4. *Collections of Decisions*, p. 388; see note 16, chapter 5.
5. *Commentary on the Criminal Code*; see note 9, chapter 7.
6. Criminal Code: Bribery.
7. *Osnovy grazhdanskogo zakonodatelstva Soyuza SSR i soyuznykh respublik* (Foundations of Civil Legislation of the USSR and Union Republics), p. 9.
8. "O nekotorykh pravilakh zapiski grazhdan" (Some Rules for the Registration of Citizens), decree by the Council of Ministers of the USSR, August 28, 1974, in *Sobranie postanovleniy pravitelstva SSSR* (Collection of Decrees by the Government of the USSR), No. 19, 1974.
9. *Sbornik opredeleniy Ugolovno-sudebnoy kollegii VS USSR* (Collection of Rulings of the Criminal Division of the Supreme Court of the Ukrainian SSR), 1924, Series V, p. 122. Quoted from Kucheryavy, *op. cit.*, p. 65; see note 1 above.
10. *Pravo i zhizn* (Law and Life), 1925, Nos. 7–8, p. 89.
11. *Sbornik opredeleniy VS RSFSR 1927g.* (Collection of Rulings by the Supreme Court of the RSFSR, 1927), p. 55. Quoted from Kucheryavy, *op. cit.*, p. 66; see note 1 above.
12. *Ugolovnoye pravo, chast osobennaya* (Criminal Law, Special Section), ed. A. A. Gertsenzon and A. K. Piontkovsky, Moscow, 1939.
13. Kucheryavy, *op. cit.*; see note 1 above.
14. *Commentary on the Criminal Code*; see note 9, chapter 7.
15. *Sbornik razyasneniy VS RSFSR za 1929* (Collection of Explanations of the Supreme Court of the RSFSR for 1929), pp. 62–63. Quoted from Kucheryavy, *op. cit.*; see note 1 above.
16. Decision by the Supreme Court of the USSR, June 24, 1949. See Criminal Code of the RSFSR, 1926, p. 23; see note 8, chapter 2.
17. Kucheryavy, *op. cit.*; see note 1 above.
18. *Ugolovnoye pravo, chast osobennaya* (Criminal Law, Special Section), ed. B. S. Utevsky, Moscow, 1958, p. 238.
19. *Collection of Decisions*; see note 16, chapter 5.
20. *Bulletin of the Supreme Court of the RSFSR*, 1962, No. 7.

9 Private Enterprise

1. Roy Medvedev, *Chto nas zhdet vperedi* (What Awaits Us), 1974, *samizdat*.

2. "Pravila registratsii nekooperirovannykh kustarey i remeslennikov" (Rules for the Registration of Domestic and Other Craftsmen not Belonging to Cooperatives), confirmed by the Council of Ministers of the USSR, June 30, 1949.

3. *Ibid.*

4. *Commentary on the Criminal Code*; see note 9, chapter 7.

5. *Collection of Decisions*, p. 348; see note 16, chapter 5.

6. A. S. Nikiforov, "Razgranichenie spekulyatsii, zanyatiya zapreshchennym promyslom i narusheniem prav torgovli," *Uchenye zapiski Vsesoyuznogo instituta yuridicheskikh nauk*, vyp. 2[6] (The Distinction between Speculation, Engaging in Prohibited Industry and Violating the Trade Laws, Bulletin of the All-Union Institute of Juridical Sciences, Series 2[6]), 1957, p. 28.

7. *Commentary on the Criminal Code*; see note 9, chapter 7.

8. Nikiforov, *op. cit.*; see note 6 above.

9. *Literaturnaya gazeta* (Literary Gazette), No. 10, 1973: A. Likhachev, article entitled "Shabashnik" (The Spare-Time Worker).

10. *Ibid.*, No. 32, 1973: Anonymous letter.

11. *Commentary on the Criminal Code*, 1964, p. 346; see note 9, chapter 7.

12. *Kurs sovetskogo ugolovnogo prava* (Course of Soviet Criminal Law), Vol. 5, pp. 433–43.

13. *Ibid.*

14. *Commentary on the Criminal Code*; see note 9, chapter 7.

15. M. G. Lyubarsky, *Kak raskryvayut tayny* (How Secrets are Discovered), Leningrad, 1968, p. 74.

16. *Zarya Vostoka* (Eastern Dawn), September 8, 1972.

17. *Collection of Decisions*; see note 16, chapter 5.

18. V. Shveisky, "Poleznaya initsiativa ili bezzakonie" (A Useful Initiative or a Lawless Act?), in *Literaturnaya gazeta* (Literary Gazette), September 5, 1973.

19. Yu. Feofanov, "Krasnaya sinka" (Red Blueprint), in *Izvestiya*, December 9, 1973.

20. Record of speech by E. K. Naumov to the People's Court of the Moskvoretsky district of the city of Moscow, 1974. Moscow, *samizdat.*

21. *Course of Soviet Criminal Law*, Vol. 5, pp. 475 ff.; see note 12 above.

22. "Ob otvetstvennosti za melkuya spekulyatsiyu" (On Responsibility for Small-Scale Speculation), ruling by the Presidium of the Supreme Court of the RSFSR, September 12, 1957: *Vedomosti RSFSR* (RSFSR Gazette), 1957, No. 1, p. 5.

23. *Course of Soviet Criminal Law*, Vol. 5, pp. 475 ff.; see note 12 above.
24. *Ibid.*
25. *Problems of Crime Prevention*, Series 15, Moscow: 1972, p. 117; see note 7, chapter 6.
26. *Ibid.*, p. 121.
27. *Collection of Decisions*, p. 348; see note 16, chapter 5.
28. S. Davitaya, "Paradoksy sada i ogoroda" (Paradoxes with Gardens and Orchards) in *Izvestiya* (News), March 22, 1973.
29. V. Mikhaylov, "Poiski pokupatelya" (In Search of a Customer), in *Izvestiya*, October 5, 1973.
30. A. Koptsov, "Khozhdenie za okroshkoy" (Looking for Cold Soup), in *Izvestiya*, May 15, 1973.
31. G. Dimov, "Osoby sluchay . . . s rediskoy" (A Special Case . . . of Radishes), in *Izvestiya*, May 13, 1973.
32. *Pravda Vostoka* (Eastern Pravda), December 17, 1960.
33. P. Voroshilov, "Raznosolnye problemy" (Pickling Problems), in *Izvestiya*, October 16, 1973.
34. G. Shcherbina, "Iz rukava v rukav" (From One Sleeve to Another), in *Izvestiya*, August 21, 1974.
35. *Commentary*; see note 9, chapter 7.

10   Theft of Socialist Property

1. K. Keny, *Osnovy ugolovnogo prava* (Foundations of Criminal Law), 1949, p. 278n.
2. G. Komrakov, "Doroga ot prokhodnoy" (The Road from the Reception Room), in *Izvestia*, January 18, 1974.
3. Order by the Ministry of Trade of the USSR, No. 102 of May 18, 1973; *cf. Izvestiya*, August 2, 1973, p. 6.
4. *Kriminologiya* (Criminology), *Yuridicheskaya literatura* (Juridical Literature), 1968, pp. 118–19.
5. V. V. Bratkovskaya, "Nekotorye voprosy uluchsheniya borby . . ." (Some Problems of Facilitating the Prevention . . .): see *Bor'ba s khishcheniyami gosudarstvennogo i obshchestvennogo imushchestva* (The Prevention of Theft of State and Public Property), collection of articles, Moscow, 1971, p. 235.
6. G. A. Kriger, *Kvalifikatsiya khishcheniya sotsialisticheskogo imushchestva* (The Definition of Theft of Socialist Property), Moscow, 1972, pp. 257 ff.
7. *Ibid.*

8. *Prevention of Theft*, p. 39; see note 5 above.
9. Lyubarsky, *op. cit.*; see note 15, chapter 9.

11 Criminal Statistics

1. Kuznetsova, *op. cit.*; see note 5, chapter 5.
2. Replevsky, "O sostoyanii prestupnosti v SSSR" (On the Existence of Crime in the USSR), in *Sotsialisticheskaya zakonnost'* (Socialist Legality), 1937, No. 11, p. 83.
3. Kuznetsova, *op. cit.*, p. 213; see note 5, chapter 5.
4. *Ibid.*, p. 187.
5. S. S. Ostroumov, *Sovetskaya sudebnaya statistika* (Soviet Judicial Statistics), Moscow, 1970, pp. 246–49.
6. *Pravda vostoka* (Eastern Pravda), December 3, 1960.
7. Kuznetsova, *op. cit.*, p. 210; see note 5, chapter 5.
8. Anashkin, "O zadachakh i tendentsiyakh razvitiya sotsialisticheskogo pravosudiya" (Problems and Trends in Soviet Jurisprudence), *Vestnik* (Bulletin) of the Law Faculty of Moscow University, 1966, No. 4.
9. *Ibid.*, p. 9.
10. *Soviet Criminology*, p. 75; see note 50, chapter 6.
11. I. I. Karpets, *Nakazanie. Sotsial'nye, pravovye i kriminologicheskiye problemy* (Punishment: Social, Legal, and Criminological Problems), Moscow, 1973, p. 118.
12. Arkady Vaksberg, "Zatmenie" (Eclipse), in *Literaturnaya gazeta* (Literary Gazette), February 20, 1974.
13. Karpets, *op. cit.*, p. 55; see note 11 above. Also Kuznetsova, *op. cit.*, p. 204; see note 5, chapter 5.

12 Prospects for the Future

1. Lenin, *Works* (3rd Russian edition), Vol. 25, p. 436.
2. Gertsenzon, *Introduction to Soviet Criminology*, p. 97; see note 33, chapter 5.
3. *Problems of Crime Prevention*, Series 1, pp. 43 ff; see note 7, chapter 6.
4. V. S. Orlov, *Podrostok i prestuplenie* (The Adolescent and Crime), Moscow, 1969; pp. 14–30.
5. *Ibid.*

6. Zagorodnikov, *op. cit.*, p. 173; see note 8, chapter 6.

7. *Osnovy zakonodatel'stva o brake i sem'ye Soyuza SSR i soyuznykh respublik* (Fundamentals of Legislation on Marriage and the Family in the USSR and Union Republics), available in English in *Fundamentals of Soviet Legislation*, Progress Publishers, Moscow, 1974.

8. "1961 Program of the Communist Party of the Soviet Union," available in English in Jan Triska, *Soviet Communism: Programs and Rules*, San Francisco: Chandler Publishing Company, 1962.

9. *Problems of Crime Prevention*, Series 3, p. 80; see note 7, chapter 6.

10. *Vsegda nacheku* (Ever on the Watch), Moscow, 1967, p. 378.

11. *Preduprezhdenie pravonarushenii sredi nesovershennoletnikh* (The Prevention of Juvenile Delinquency), Minsk, 1969, p. 51.

12. *Ibid.*, p. 12.

13. *The Prevention of Juvenile Crime*, p. 190; see note 19, chapter 5.

14. Chalidze, *op. cit.*; see note 5, chapter 2.

15. Orlov, *op. cit.*, p. 36; see note 4 above.

16. *Ibid.*, p. 142.

17. *Juvenile Delinquency*, p. 10; see note 11 above.

18. *Ibid.*

Index

About the Author

VALERY CHALIDZE, author of *To Defend These Rights*, an investigation of the status of civil liberties in the USSR, was born in Moscow in 1938. He was co-founder of the Moscow Human Rights Committee and edited and *signed* fifteen issues of the *samizdat* journal *Social Problems*. In November 1972 he came to the United States to lecture at Georgetown University. Because of his active defense of human rights and civil liberties in the Soviet Union, he was deprived of his citizenship and refused re-entry to Russia. He now lives in New York City and is editor of *A Chronicle of Human Rights in the USSR*, a bimonthly journal which reports on the human rights movement in the Soviet Union.

DATE DUE